100 GREATEST SPORTSPERSONS

Kalyani Mookherji is an alumnus of Jadavpur University, Kolkata, from where she finished her post-graduation in English Literature. She has been a writer and educator for over ten years now. She also runs a popular literary workshop for children, Feeling Bookerish, in Wellington, a town in The Nilgiris District of the Indian state of Tamil Nadu, where she currently resides after having travelled the length and breadth of India as an army wife.

Her childhood love for the sport of cycling and current penchant for hiking along the lush green Nilgiri trails, inspired her to write this book about sports.

Despite being a busy mom to a bright teen and a spoilt dog, she finds time for other interests such as music, baking and blogging at crumbsonmynotebook.wordpress.com

100 GREATEST SPORTSPERSONS

Kalyani Mookherji

RUPA

Published by
Rupa Publications India Pvt. Ltd 2018
7/16, Ansari Road, Daryaganj
New Delhi 110002

Sales Centres:
Allahabad Bengaluru Chennai
Hyderabad Jaipur Kathmandu
Kolkata Mumbai

Copyright © Kalyani Mookherji 2018

The views and opinions expressed in this book are the author's own and the facts
are as reported by her which have been verified to the extent possible,
and the publishers are not in any way liable for the same.

All rights reserved.
No part of this publication may be reproduced, transmitted,
or stored in a retrieval system, in any form or by any means, electronic,
mechanical, photocopying, recording or otherwise,
without the prior permission of the publisher.

ISBN: 978-93-5304-073-4

Second impression 2019

10 9 8 7 6 5 4 3 2

The moral right of the author has been asserted.

Printed at HT Media Ltd, Noida

This book is sold subject to the condition that it shall not, by way of trade
or otherwise, be lent, resold, hired out, or otherwise circulated, without the
publisher's prior consent, in any form of binding or cover other than that in
which it is published.

23.	Dhyan Chand	56
24.	Diego Maradona	59
25.	Don Bradman	62
26.	Eddy Merckx	64
27.	Edwin Moses	67
28.	Emil Zátopek	69
29.	Fanny Blankers-Koen	72
30.	Gareth Edwards	75
31.	Garfield Sobers	77
32.	Greg Louganis	80
33.	Haile Gebrselassie	82
34.	Heather McKay	84
35.	Hicham El Guerrouj	86
36.	Ian Botham	89
37.	Ian Thorpe	91
38.	Imran Khan	94
39.	Jack Nicklaus	96
40.	Jackie Joyner-Kersee	99
41.	Jahangir Khan	102
42.	Jesse Owens	105
43.	Joe Frazier	108
44.	Joe Montana	110
45.	Kareem Abdul-Jabbar	112
46.	Katie Ledecky	115
47.	Kelly Slater	117
48.	Larisa Latynina	120
49.	Leander Paes	123
50.	Lee Chong Wei	126
51.	Lin Dan	128
52.	Lionel Messi	131
53.	Magic Johnson	134

CONTENTS

Introduction ix

1.	Abebe Bikila	1
2.	Abhinav Bindra	3
3.	Alexander Karelin	6
4.	Alexander Popov	8
5.	Annika Sorenstam	10
6.	Ayrton Senna	13
7.	Babe D. Zaharias	15
8.	Babe Ruth	18
9.	Ben Ainslie	21
10.	Bernard Hinault	23
11.	Billie Jean King	25
12.	Birgit Fischer	28
13.	Björn Borg	30
14.	Bob Mathias	33
15.	Bobby Jones	36
16.	Bobby Moore	38
17.	Boris Becker	41
18.	Brian Lara	44
19.	Carl Lewis	47
20.	Colin Meads	49
21.	Daley Thompson	51
22.	David Beckham	53

54.	Ma Long	136
55.	Mark Spitz	138
56.	Martina Navratilova	141
57.	M.C. Mary Kom	144
58.	Michael Johnson	147
59.	Michael Jordan	149
60.	Michael Phelps	152
61.	Michael Schumacher	154
62.	Mike Tyson	157
63.	Milkha Singh	160
64.	Muhammad Ali	162
65.	Nadia Comaneci	165
66.	Natalie Coughlin	168
67.	Paavo Nurmi	171
68.	Pele	174
69.	Pete Sampras	176
70.	Pullela Gopichand	178
71.	P.T. Usha	180
72.	Pyrros Dimas	182
73.	Rafael Nadal	184
74.	Rod Laver	186
75.	Roger Bannister	189
76.	Roger Federer	191
77.	Sachin Tendulkar	193
78.	Serena Williams	196
79.	Shane Warne	198
80.	Shaun White	201
81.	Steffi Graf	203
82.	Steve Redgrave	206
83.	Sunil Gavaskar	208
84.	Sania Mirza	210

85.	Sergey Bubka	213
86.	Sushil Kumar	215
87.	Saina Nehwal	217
88.	Tiger Woods	220
89.	Usain Bolt	223
90.	Valentino Rossi	226
91.	Vijender Singh	229
92.	Viv Richards	232
93.	Wang Nan	234
94.	Wayne Gretzky	236
95.	Willie Mays	238
96.	Willie Shoemaker	241
97.	Wu Minxia	243
98.	Yelena Isinbayeva	245
99.	Zinedine Zidane	248
100.	Zhang Ning	251

Conclusion 253
Acknowledgements 254

INTRODUCTION

'Sports are a microcosm of society.'

This quote by women's tennis icon Billie Jean King is a pithy indicator of the many reasons why sports rouse people across the world. Sports speak to the innate human impulse to beat the odds and overcome obstacles. They bring a community together, as supporters root for their own teams, while, at the same time, legendary players can demolish national, linguistic, class and other such barriers through the global adulation they inspire.

However, some writers such as George Orwell have struck a more sombre note, suggesting that sports probably act as a modern-day substitute for wars since the ancient urge for bloodlust and violence can thus be channeled in safer ways. Even then, sports have a lot to teach humanity. Respect for fundamental rules, learning to work as a team, and above all, upholding values such as fair play and equality, are ingrained in all sports. Indeed, in fractured times, such as those of economic depression or natural disasters, when a community has little to look forward to, success in sports can give people something to cheer about.

Inspired by humanity's timeless and universal love for sports, this book takes on the ambitious task of restricting its modern heroes to 100 names. The criteria for inclusion are not just professional and monetary success in a particular sport but also, more importantly, the legacy of the sportsperson—the ways in which he or she has helped the game to grow and transform. Again, there has been a genuine attempt to make the names as representative as possible and therefore, while widely popular sports such as football and tennis have their icons, trailblazers of sports with limited global presence, such as jockeying, sailing and ice-hockey, have not been forgotten. Motivation has been another significant concern while selecting the names since certain sportspersons may have played a greater role in popularizing a particular sport, or the culture of sports in general, in a community, rather than attaining conventional success in terms of records and medals.

So, here you go—the brightest 100 names from the world of sports, who, by sheer hard work and determination, went on to make history!

ABEBE BIKILA

One of the reasons why sports inspire people the world over is because they set a level playing field for all competitors—and, every once in a while, up comes a winner about whom the world would not have known otherwise. Ethiopian marathon runner Abebe Bikila is just such a name in the history of athletics. Running barefoot at the 1960 Olympic Games in Rome, Bikila not only set the world record for the fastest timing but also became the first black African to win an Olympic gold.

Abebe Bikila was born in Ethiopia to a family of shepherds. As a young man, Bikila was recruited into the army of Ethiopian Emperor Haille Selassie, as part of the royal bodyguards. It was at a training camp where Bikila's talent for long-distance running was spotted by Swedish coach, Onni Niskanen, who groomed him for competitive running.

Eventually, Bikila found himself in Rome for the 1960 Olympics. Though for the greater part of the race Bikila appeared to be running neck and neck alongside the Moroccan runner Rhadi Ben Abdesselam, in the last 1,000 metres he managed to break ahead and cross the finish line at the Arch of Constantine. With a timing of 2 hours 15 minutes and 16.2 seconds, Bikila had set a new world record, along with becoming the first black African sportsperson to win a gold medal at the Olympic Games.

Four years later—a mere forty days before the start of the 1964 Tokyo Olympics—the world of athletics was alarmed to learn about Bikila undergoing surgery for the treatment of appendicitis. It seemed very doubtful that he would recover in time for the Games. However, Bikila not only disproved the naysayers but stunned the sporting world by winning yet another gold medal and setting a new world record of 2 hours 12 minutes and 11.2 seconds, thus becoming the first athlete in the world to win two Olympic marathons.

Though Bikila entered the 1968 Olympics in Mexico City, he suffered an injury ten miles into the marathon and was forced to drop out of the event. Apart from receiving worldwide honours such as the BBC 'Overseas Sports Personality of the Year' award in 1964, he was honoured in his own country by being promoted to the rank of Captain of the palace guard. In 1969 however, a motor accident left Bikila a paraplegic and a few years later he died from a brain haemorrhage in 1973. Upon his death, Emperor Haile Selassie proclaimed a national day of mourning in remembrance of an amazing runner blessed with natural grace and stamina, whose career included fifteen marathon races and as many as twelve victories. Bikila's achievements went on to inspire other East African runners such as Haile Gebrselassie, Mamo Wolde, Juma Ikangaa, Tegla Loroupe and Paul Tergat.

- In the 1960 Olympics, Bikila decided to run the marathon without shoes, just as he was used to in his own country.

- In the aftermath of a rebellion at the Emperor's palace, Bikila's life was in danger but he escaped death because of the Emperor's personal intervention.

ABHINAV BINDRA

Abhinav Bindra is a gold medallist in the Olympic Games as well as in the World Championship in the 10 metre Air Rifle event. He is most famous for being the first Indian to win an individual gold medal in the Olympic Games when he topped the 10 metre Air Rifle event in Beijing in 2008.

Born on 28 September 1982 in Dehradun, Bindra, right from his childhood, displayed single-minded determination which would eventually help him on his way to the Olympic gold. Such was his devotion to the sport, that his parents had an indoor shooting range installed at their home in Patiala in the north Indian state of Punjab. Bindra received his earliest coaching from Lt. Col. Dhillon and later his shooting skills were honed under the watchful guidance of Dr Amit Bhattacharjee.

In the year 2000, Bindra became the youngest participant of the Indian Olympic contingent in Sydney. However, his performance was disheartening as he ended up in the 11th position in the qualifying rankings of the 10 metre Air Rifle event. Since 2001 however, Bindra seemed to have found his form as he won the bronze medal in the International Shooting Sport Federation (ISSF) Cup hosted in Munich that year. In 2002, at the Commonwealth Games in Manchester, he won the gold medal in the pairs event as well as the individual silver medal. Next year, he once again retained the bronze medal at the Munich ISSF. In the 2006 Melbourne Commonwealth Games, the performance of the previous meet was repeated as he came back with the gold medal in the pairs event and the individual silver medal. The same year, Bindra seized the gold medal at the 2006 ISSF World Championship and this heralded the best phase of his career.

Bindra reached the pinnacle of his sporting career in 2008 when he won the 10 metre Air Rifle event in Beijing Olympics, thus becoming the first Indian in the country's sporting history to bring back an individual gold medal. Interestingly, at the qualifying round in Beijing, he had come 4th, but then his rock-solid performance earned him a score of 104.5 in the final round, with which he set a new record for his country.

In the 2010 Commonwealth Games held in New Delhi, Bindra earned a silver medal in the individual event as well as a gold in the pairs event. However, four years later, he again proved his mettle with an individual gold medal at the 2014 Commonwealth Games in Glasgow. The same year, he brought home two bronze medals from the Asian Games held at Incheon—one in the individual capacity and the other as part of the team.

Two years later, Bindra was sent to Rio as the Goodwill Ambassador of the 2016 Olympic Games Indian contingent but was unable to win any medal. The shortfall of a mere 0.1 point placed him at the 4th place in the final of the men's 10 metre Air Rifle event with a cumulative score of 163.8. After returning from the 2016 Olympic Games, Bindra announced his retirement from competitive shooting. However, his association with the sport continues through the Abhinav Bindra Shooting Development Programme that he launched to support India's youngsters with shooting potential.

In recognition for the glory that Bindra brought India, he has been honoured with a series of awards, including the Arjuna Award in 2000, the Rajiv Gandhi Khel Ratna award—the highest

State award for sporting excellence in India—in 2001, and the Padma Bhushan—the country's third-highest civilian award—in 2009.

- At the age of fifteen, Bindra was the youngest participant in the 1998 Commonwealth Games.
- In the 2016 Olympics, just before the start of the 10 metre Air Rifle qualification, Bindra fell down, along with his gun, from the chair on which he was sitting, as a result of which the sight of his rifle broke.

ALEXANDER KARELIN

Alexander Karelin is a Russian Greco-Roman wrestler who is considered the most successful exponent of this form of wrestling in modern history. The winner of three Olympic gold medals, twelve European Championships and nine World Championships, Karelin ruled the sport for thirteen years, never losing even one match in all this while. In fact, for ten years of this period, he did not even concede a single point to an opponent.

Born in Novobirsk, Siberia, Karelin grew up amidst the rigours of a harsh climate which, in turn, built up his stamina as well as determination to overcome all odds. After experimenting with various sports such as weightlifting, boxing, basketball, volleyball and skiing, he decided to take up wrestling and found a lifelong coach in Viktor Kuznetsov.

Karelin's winning streak began in 1988, when he earned the European Championships title and made a place for himself in the Russian super-heavyweight wrestling team that was to go to Seoul for the Olympics. There he won the gold medal and continued to defend his Olympic title for the next two Games at Barcelona in 1992 and then at Atlanta in 1996—thus setting a record for three successive Olympic gold medals in the super-heavyweight wrestling event.

Karelin's Olympic glory was suitably complemented by his complete dominance in other championships. For nine consecutive years, from 1988–96, and later in 1998, 1999 and 2000, he was the winner of the European Championships. He also seized the World Championship title from 1989 to 1991, then again from 1993 to 1995 and in the final phase from 1997 to 1999.

In 2000 however, Karelin had to settle for the silver medal at the Sydney Olympics and despite winning the European Championships that year, retired from the sport.

In 2007, Karelin was elected to the Russian parliament as a representative of the Stavropol Krai and he continues to be a member of Duma's committee on international affairs.

Alexander Karelin's undisputed reign in the world of super-heavyweight wrestling gave him a sort of demi-god status in his home country. Variously hailed as 'Alexander the Great', the 'Russian Bear', 'Russian King Kong' and 'The Experiment', today he is regarded as the greatest Greco-Roman wrestler of all time.

- Karelin has the distinction of being the flag bearer at three consecutive Olympics, each time for a different national entity–in 1988 for the Soviet Union, in 1992 for the Unified Team and finally for Russia in 1996.

- One famous anecdote about Karelin's immense strength is that he once carried–all by himself–a refrigerator eight floors to his apartment.

ALEXANDER POPOV

Russian swimmer Alexander Popov is considered the greatest sprint swimmer in the history of the sport. In the 1992 Olympics, he won two gold medals for 50 metre and 100 metre freestyle swimming—a feat that he repeated at the 1996 Olympic Games—thus becoming the only male swimmer in Olympic history to have successfully defended both titles.

Born as Aleksandr Vladimirovich Popov on 16 November 1971 in Russia, the future swimming icon first entered the pool when he was eight and that too, when his father decided that this was the only way to get the child to overcome his fear of water. Initially, Popov swam the backstroke, but after famed Russian swimming coach Gennadi Touretski accepted the youngster into his squad in 1990, he pointed out that Popov's freestyle technique held more potential.

Though Popov had to move to Australia to be coached by Touretski, the decision helped his career and he qualified for the 1992 Barcelona Olympics. There, Popov swept away the sprint swimming event, winning gold medals both in the 50 metre as well as in the 100 metre competitions.

Four years later at the Atlanta Olympics in 1996, Popov defended both the 50 metre and the 100 metre titles and again won two gold medals. Grateful for the guidance received during his stint at the Australian Swimming Institute, he presented the 100 metre gold medal won at Atlanta to his coach, Touretski.

Popov's Olympic high was broken by an unfortunate incident in 1996 when, just a month after the Games, he was stabbed during a street brawl in Moscow. The injuries to his kidney and lung were serious enough to warrant an emergency surgery and a gruelling three-month rehabilitation.

Despite the grievous attack, Popov ensured a steady return to form. The very next year he successfully defended his 50 metre and 100 metre freestyle titles at the 1997 European Championships in Seville, Spain. In the 2003 Barcelona World Championships, Popov once again made a clean sweep of his specialities—the 50 metre and 100 metre sprint swimming events. While being felicitated for his victories, Popov remarked that Barcelona would always be special to him as it was here that he had tasted Olympic success for the first time at the 1992 Games.

Unknown to Popov, this would also be his swan song, as next year, the Russian swimmer could not even qualify in the 2004 Athens Olympics. Not surprisingly, shortly afterwards he announced his retirement from active swimming in January 2005.

Known for his long, graceful strokes, Popov ruled the 50 metre and 100 metre freestyle events in the 1990s and today he is regarded as the finest sprint swimmer of all times.

- The 1996 stabbing incident brought a new-found appreciation of life's priorities and shortly afterwards, Popov decided to go for a baptism ceremony at a Russian Orthodox Church and the following spring, he got married to his sweetheart.

- One of Popov's techniques is to make his enemies nervous; he says, 'If I see any (challenger), I have to swim faster and make them feel sick.'

ANNIKA SORENSTAM

Swedish golfer Annika Sorenstam is feted as one of the most famous female golfers in the history of the sport. With a staggering seventy-two Ladies Professional Golf Association (LPGA) events and ten major championships under her belt, and as the only woman to break 60 in an official event, Sorenstam has convinced the golfing world to take a fresh look at its female players.

Sorenstam was born on 9 October 1970, in Stockholm, Sweden, into a family that enjoyed and encouraged sports. Initially, her affinities lay towards tennis; when she was just five, she competed in her first tennis tournament. However, by the time she turned sixteen, golf had replaced tennis as her primary interest.

In 1990, Sorenstam arrived at Tucson on an athletics scholarship to the University of Arizona and soon caught the sporting community's attention by winning the National Collegiate Athletic Association (NCAA) golf championship in her freshman year. For this feat, she was honoured as 'College Player of the Year'.

Sorenstam started playing professionally in 1993 when she qualified for the European Women's Tour. The next year, she qualified for the LPGA event and both in 1993 and 1994, she was awarded the title of 'Rookie of the Year'. In 1995, Sorenstam won the most prestigious tournament in women's golf—US Women's Open—and the same year, she received the Vare Trophy, awarded to the player with the lowest scoring average of the season. For her achievements in 1995, Sorenstam was honoured with the title of LPGA 'Player of the Year'.

After taking a short break from professional golf, Sorenstam returned to the course in 1996 to lift the Women's Open, as well as the Vare, trophies, for the second time. Unfortunately, in 1997, she could not defend either title though she finished the year with six tournament victories. Next year, however, she won back the Vare Trophy as well as five other championships. After a dull 1999, Sorenstam returned to top form in 2000, when she won five championships.

In 2003, Sorenstam took the world media by storm when she joined the male golfers at the 2003 Colonial Invitational in Fort Worth, Texas, thus becoming the first woman to play in a Professional Golfers' Association (PGA) Tour event in fifty-eight years. Though she was unable to make the final cut, the experience not only left her feeling stronger but was a milestone in the history of women's sports. In recognition of this achievement as well as for her three of the four major LPGA tournament wins, Sorenstam was inducted into the World Golf Hall of Fame in 2003, thus setting the record for the youngest person to be admitted to the Hall.

After the 2008 season, Sorenstam retired from professional golf to spend more time with her family as well as to look after her business label, titled ANNIKA, which along with The ANNIKA Foundation, promotes a healthy lifestyle among children.

- During a press conference before the men's 2005 US Open, Tiger Woods talked about emulating legends such as Jack Nicklaus, Arnold Palmer and Lee Trevino.

    'Do you ever emulate Annika?' a reporter yelled out.

    'If I could only hit it that straight, man...' replied Woods, cracking a smile.

- Sorenstam's favourite karaoke song is 'Winner Takes it All' by ABBA, a Swedish pop group.

AYRTON SENNA

Brazilian motorcar-racing legend, Ayrton Senna, was a three-time Formula One (F1) Champion and had forty-one Grand Prix wins to his name. Senna was killed in a crash in Bologna, Italy, where he was leading the 1994 San Marino Grand Prix.

Born as Ayrton Senna da Silva on 21 March 1960 into a well-off family of Sao Paulo, Brazil, the future racer was initially interested in go-cart racing and even won the South American Kart Championship in 1977. From 1978 to 1982, he would go on to compete in the Karting World Championship each year, ending up as the runner-up in 1979 as well as 1980.

After short successful stints in the Formula Ford as well as Formula Three (F3) Championships, Senna made his debut into the F1 circuit at the 1984 Brazilian Grand Prix at Interlagos. However, because of his association with the second-tier Toleman team, Senna proved less than successful. A stellar performance by Senna at the Monaco Grand Prix despite car troubles, prompted Team Lotus to buy out the Brazilian racer from Toleman. Senna didn't let them down by winning his first F1 Grand Prix at Estoril.

Following this win, Senna moved on to the McLaren team for whom he won the F1 Championships for three years—1988, 1990 and 1991. However, at McLaren, Senna also got embroiled in a long rivalry with French teammate Alain Prost. Though Senna could not defend his F1 Championship title in 1992, the next year he managed to win five races and finished the season as a runner-up.

In 1994, Senna managed to move on to the then highly successful Williams team but his performance that season suffered from the several changes in the rules of F1 racing and the resultant uncertainties. On 1 May 1994, as Senna took the lead in the final race at the San Marino Grand Prix, his car swerved into a concrete wall when turning a curve and the resultant injuries proved fatal.

Ayrton Senna is still remembered as one of the greatest among F1 drivers. He not only seized the F1 Championship titles three times but also won the Monaco Grand Prix a record six times, besides winning forty-one races and sixty-five pole positions in a career that ended prematurely. Famed for victories in wet weather conditions, Senna was marked by the unquenchable desire to push further.

- After a race in 1993, Senna got into an argument with Irishman Eddie Irvine, upon which the Brazilian punched Irvine in the face.

- Senna once said, 'I am not designed to come second or third. I am designed to win.'

BABE D. ZAHARIAS

While it was tough to be a successful female athlete during the middle of the last century, it was even more remarkable to garner laurels in multiple sports. But that is what Babe D. Zaharias managed to do, when in 1950, she was crowned as 'The Woman Athlete of the Half Century' for her sporting achievements in track and field, basketball and golf.

Born as Mildred Ella Didrikson on 26 June 1911, in Port Arthur, Texas, the future women's athletics icon was brought up in a Norwegian immigrant family which placed great emphasis on physical fitness and sporting temperament. Add to that her own talent for various sports and as early as high school, she began excelling on the courts.

Zaharias's first major run of sporting success came with her employment at the Dallas-based Employer's Casualty Company where she was on its basketball, baseball, diving, tennis as well as track and field teams. For three successive years—1930, 1931 and 1932—Zaharias led the company's basketball team to the national championship because of which she was chosen as a National Women's Amateur Athletic Union (AAU) All-American forward for the Women's National Basketball League for all three years. More importantly, at the 1931 National AAU Track Meet, which was the qualifying meet for the Olympics next year, Zaharias won gold medals in five out of ten events and tied for gold in a sixth. She set world records in the javelin, 80 metre hurdles, high jump and baseball throw. Next year, Zaharias swept the national AAU championships and single-handedly won the team championships.

However, the greatest moment of her sporting glory came during the 1932 Los Angeles Olympics. She finished the Games with a gold medal in javelin throw and in 80 metre hurdles, and a silver medal both in high jump.

As if so many different sports were not enough, Zaharias took up golf in the early 1930s and by April 1935, she had become expert enough to win the Texas State Women's Championship two-up. However, the same year, she lost her amateur status in the US Golf Association (USGA) after having commercially endorsed an automobile company. In the wake of this expulsion, she took to playing exhibition golf and for the next several years, made money from various travelling vaudeville acts. In December 1938, she married Greek wrestler George Zaharias who encouraged her to apply for reinstatement as an amateur golfer and eventually in January 1943, she was allowed to get back to the USGA circuit. Merely four years later, Zaharias won the British Ladies' Amateur Championship, at Gullane, Scotland, thus becoming the first American woman to do so.

In August 1947, however, Zaharias decided to turn professional and for the next six years, dominated women's golf, despite undergoing surgery when she was diagnosed with cancer. In 1954, she even won the US Women's Open by twelve strokes but succumbed to the disease the year after.

Today, Babe Didrikson Zaharias is regarded as a pioneer of modern-day women's sports. With her immense talent, unwavering perseverance and steely ambition to succeed, she not only broke world sporting records but also long-entrenched gender stereotypes about what it was to be a successful woman and sportsperson.

- As the youngest in her family, Mildred was called 'Baby'; once during a baseball game, she hit five home runs which resulted in her brothers renaming her 'Babe' after the then baseball star Babe Ruth–a nickname she would keep for the rest of her life.

- In the 1932 Olympics, women were only allowed to enter three events since they were considered too weak to compete in more than that number. Despite this unfair limitation, Zaharias broke four world records.

BABE RUTH

George Herman Ruth is regarded the world over as a veritable legend in the history of baseball. Many of the former American player's personal achievements—such as highest slugging percentage for a season, most total bases in a season and most years leading a league in home runs—are yet to be matched. Even more significantly, Ruth's personal and professional success redefined baseball from casual recreation to a sport promising stardom to the best.

Though Ruth's exact date of birth is still a topic of dispute among some sports historians, it is generally agreed that he was born in February 1895 in Baltimore, Maryland, into a family of modest means. For the greater part of his childhood, he lived at the St. Mary's Industrial School for Boys, which housed orphans and juvenile offenders. It was here that Ruth encountered Brother Mathias, who, despite being a stickler for discipline, motivated Ruth to focus on baseball. And still playing for St. Mary's team, the teenaged Ruth became famous in and around Baltimore as the next baseball sensation.

On 27 February 1914, nineteen-year-old Ruth made his professional debut with the Baltimore Orioles. As the youngest player of the team, he was called 'Babe' by his mates, but as he became more popular, the moniker began to be used by others as well. Ruth led the Orioles to victory fourteen times and to the height of the International League rankings. However, the club's financial trouble saw Ruth being traded to Boston Red Sox in 1914 though it would be only in the next season that he would get to be a full-fledged member of the team.

In 1915, Red Sox won the World Series and over the next five years, Ruth's destructive pitching led the team to three championship titles. The highlight, most definitely, was the 1916 championship which saw Ruth pitch for thirteen innings without allowing a single hitter to score in even one game—an achievement which continues to be unmatched.

As a hitter, too, Ruth grew in stature. While batting .322, he hit a record 29 home runs and drove in 114 runs. In the 1918 season especially, he drove crowds wild with 4 home runs on loaded bases that were celebrated as 'grand slams'.

After returning from mandatory military service during the First World War, Ruth was transferred again—this time to New York Yankees—at the close of 1919. From 1920 onwards, he dominated the world of baseball like no one before—or ever since. In 1920, Ruth became the first player to hit 30, 40 and 50 home runs in a season which ended with .376 average and a total of 54 home runs and 137 runs batted in (RBIs). His most successful season, though, would be 1921, which would see his batting average shoot to .378 and a staggering total of 59 home runs and 171 runs. In the 1923 season, Ruth smashed 41 home runs—the league highest—and the next season, he led the Yankees to a 4–2 World Championship Series win for which he was nicknamed the 'Sultan of Swat'.

Though plagued by fitness issues in 1925, Ruth bounced back the following year. Over the next seven seasons, he batted at .353 while accumulating 151 RBIs and an average of 49 home runs. In 1927, Ruth set a world record by hitting 60 home runs—the most in a single season. It would be another thirty-four years before anyone would be able to match the feat.

In 1935, Ruth played his last pro match and the next year, he was one of the first five players to be welcomed into the Baseball Hall of Fame. Though after retirement he took up a coaching job at Brooklyn Dodgers, his heart was not in it. On 16 August 1948, the legendary baseball player succumbed to a long struggle with cancer. Even after passing away, Ruth's memory was honoured time and again—his name was included in the Major League All-Century Team, along with being feted as the 'Athlete of the Century' by the Associated Press as well as the 'Greatest Player of All Time' by *The Sporting News*.

- In 1930, Ruth reportedly signed a two-year, $80,000-per-year contract that was touted to be higher than even the then pay of the President of the United States.

- In 1923, the New York Yankee Stadium was nicknamed 'The House that Ruth Built'.

BEN AINSLIE

Ben Ainslie is perhaps the most famous name in modern competitive sailing. British by birth and with the formal title of Sir Charles Benedict Ainslie, he is the winner of the highest number of Olympic medals—four gold medals and one silver.

Ainslie was born on 5 February 1977 in Macclesfield, Cheshire, England but seven years later his family moved to the coast of Cornwall, where he first attempted to sail on the waters of Restronguet Creek in an Optimist (a small dinghy) as a mere nine-year-old. Fortunately for Ainslie, both his parents were keen sailors and thus he had all the guidance required within the family. Not surprisingly then, by the time he turned sixteen, Ainslie had already seized the Laser Radial world as well as the European Championships titles.

Ainslie made his Olympic debut at Atlanta in 1996 when the Laser class was included for the first time in the Games. Though he had to settle for the silver, the Atlanta Olympics proved to the world that Ainslie was a champion in the making. Over the next four Games, Ainslie won gold medals—the first of these was in the Laser class at the 2000 Sydney Olympics after which he moved onto the heavier Finn class in which he won gold medals at the 2004 Athens Olympics, the 2008 Beijing Olympics and finally at the 2012 London Olympics.

Apart from the Olympics, Ainslie has proved his mettle in the single-handed Laser and Finn classes where he was the world champion for a staggering nine times, besides seizing a World Match Racing Tour title too. Though Ainslie's appearances in the America's Cup series were not as consistently successful as in the Olympics, in June 2013 his team competed in the Round the Island Race, off the Isle of Wright, and breezed past the standing multihull record by more than 16 minutes. For all his achievements, Ainslie was honoured with the International Sailing Federation (ISAF) 'Sailor of the Year' title three times—in 1999, 2002 and 2008—besides being conferred a knighthood in the 2013 New Year Honours list.

Known for his highly competitive racing style, which his detractors have even gone so far as to describe as aggressive, Ainslie has occasionally been at the receiving end of disqualification rules. However, with his sheer power and careful manoeuvring tactics, Ainslie has proved himself the greatest competitive sailor in the modern history of the sport.

- For the men's single-handed Finn class event for sailing, at the Olympics in 2004, Ainslie reportedly had to add around 15 kg of muscle to his frame.

- In 2011, at the end of a race, Ainslie dived off his boat to confront the driver of a media boat, leading to his disqualification.

BERNARD HINAULT

Bernard is a former cyclist who is famous for his five Tour de France championship titles and is best known as the last Frenchman to win the prestigious Tour de France. With a staggering two hundred victories during twelve years of competitive cycling, he has reserved his place among the greatest professional cyclists of all times.

Born on 14 November 1954 in Brittany, France, into a farming family, Hinault was not greatly attracted to cycling in his childhood. It was only after he received a bicycle as a present upon finishing school, that he began riding and, motivated by the company of a cousin who was a cycling enthusiast, discovered his life goal.

Hinault made his debut as a professional cyclist in 1974, though it would be another four years before he would acquire the necessary training to compete in the Tour de France. His first grand tour was the Vuelta a España in 1978 which he won along with the national championships that year. Consequently, he felt confident enough to compete in the Tour de France in 1978. The long years of preparation bore fruit and Hinault won the Tour de France on his debut attempt. He would go on to win the gruelling competition another four times—in 1979, 1981, 1982 and 1985. Apart from the Tour, he would claim the Vuelta championship title once more in 1983 as well as the Giro d' Italia three times—in 1980, 1982 and 1985. Hinault retired shortly afterwards, at the relatively young age of thirty-two.

In the course of his career in competitive cycling, Hinault won ten Grand Tour titles—just one short of the maximum number of such titles that is held by Belgian cycling legend Eddie Merckx (a record eleven). Even then, Hinault's achievements are in a class of their own. In 1984 and 1986, he finished second in the Tour de France competitions which makes him the only cyclist in the history of professional cycling to have figured in the top two positions at every Tour de France event that he has competed in.

Bernard has been hailed not only because of his championship titles but also due to the diversity of his cycling skills, such as sprint, time trial and climb, which contributed to his victories at all the classifications of the Tour. Towards the middle of his career, his popularity was marginally dimmed on account of his perceived aggression on the cycling circuits as well as outspokenness off it, which did not sit well with the authorities and the media. Eventually though, Hinault's reputation recovered and today, he is regarded as one of the greatest cyclists of the twentieth century.

- Hinault was affectionately nicknamed 'Le Blaireau', meaning 'The Badger'.
- A much coveted aspect of the Tour de France is the yellow jersey worn by the rider with the fastest overall time from the very start of the first day of the race. Hinault was the recipient of the same, several times.

BILLIE JEAN KING

In the battle to win, the sports arena often becomes a metaphor for the fight for self-respect and equality. This is particularly true in case of women's tennis icon, Billie Jean King, who was not only the top-ranked women's tennis player by 1967, but throughout her career, strove to break down barriers of gender and sexuality.

Billie Jean King was born on 22 November 1943, in Long Beach, California, into a family of competent sportspersons. By the age of eleven, Billie Jean herself was playing tennis on public courts of Long Island, and in 1958, won the Southern California Championship in her age group.

Billie Jean's first international triumph came in 1961 when, with Karen Hantze Susman, she won the Wimbledon women's doubles title—the youngest pair to do so. However, rising to the top in singles proved to be more difficult. After marriage to law student Larry King, Billie Jean started training harder. And her efforts paid off when in 1966, she won her first major singles championship at Wimbledon.

After this, there was no stopping this tennis star whose speed, back-hand expertise and net-game, catapulted her to the top of the ranks. Billie Jean continued to defend her Wimbledon singles title in 1967 and 1968 while also winning the US Open singles in 1967 as well as the Australian Open in 1968. After turning professional in 1968, Billie Jean continued her trailblazing performance in singles, doubles and mixed-doubles tournaments through the following years. 1972 particularly proved to be a fantastic year as she swept away three Grand Slam titles with her wins in the US Open, French Open and Wimbledon.

Along with championship titles poured in financial rewards and in 1971, Billie Jean became the first female athlete to make more than $100,000 in prize money in a single year. Even then, she asserted the right of female tennis players to be paid the same prize money as their male counterparts as Billie Jean believed that women, in any field, are as efficient, hardworking and talented as their male counterparts. With this in mind, she formed the Women's Tennis Association in 1973 and the same year, she threatened to boycott the 1973 US Open if the pay inequality was not rectified. The organizers buckled and the US Open became the first major tournament to award equal prize money to female and male players—largely because of Billie Jean's unwavering courage.

1975 to 1977 marked a brief hiatus from singles tennis for Billie Jean. However, once she came back, she started a winning spree at Wimbledon till 1983. Though she is best known for her record twenty Wimbledon titles, in all, Billie Jean won thirty-nine major singles, doubles and mixed-doubles championships.

In her personal life, Billie Jean was as assertive as on the tennis courts. In 1981, she became the first famous female sportsperson to publicly admit to a lesbian relationship. Though she lost many endorsement contracts and had to go through a divorce in 1987, Billie Jean emerged a pioneer for the rights of female athletes and the LGBT community. Her efforts were formally recognized in 2009 when she received the Presidential Medal of Freedom from then President, Barack Obama.

- A highlight of Billie Jean's career was her win in the much-hyped 'Battle of the Sexes' in which–watched by 50 million TV viewers–she defeated Bobby Riggs who had won the Wimbledon men's singles, doubles and mixed-doubles titles in 1939.

- As a nod to Billie Jean's World TeamTennis, friend and singer Elton John wrote a song, 'Philadelphia Freedom', which was released on New Year's Day (1975) and went on to become a big hit.

BIRGIT FISCHER

If it is a challenge for female athletes to be the best at a sport, it is an even bigger achievement if they are able to do it in an unusual sport. But that is just what Birgit Fischer accomplished. As the winner of a total of eight Olympic gold medals, she is the most famous kayaker in the world and an inspiration to women across the globe to explore new sporting activities.

Fischer was born on 25 February 1962, at Brandenburg an der Havel, which was then part of East Germany. While growing up, she was coached at the Army Sports Club in Potsdam and later became a coach at the same institute. Of her six Olympic appearances, Fischer represented East Germany twice, and the other four times, she competed on behalf of Unified Germany. By seizing one gold in the 1980 Moscow Olympics in the K-1 500 metre kayaking event, she set the tone for an amazing career that would go on to include a double gold in 1988 at Seoul, then another gold in 1992 at Barcelona, followed by a gold in Atlanta 1996, again a double gold in 2000 at Sydney, and finally a gold in 2004 at Athens Olympics—thus bringing her overall Olympic tally to eight gold medals.

Fischer shared her record eight Olympic gold medals with Hungarian fencer Aladar Gerevich, but while in her case they came from six Olympic appearances, in case of the latter, they were distributed over seven Olympic Games. Twice, after the 1996 and the 2000 Olympic Games, Fischer announced her retirement from competitive kayaking, only to make a comeback.

Apart from a stellar Olympic career, Fischer has also dominated the International Canoe Federation (ICF) Canoe Sprint World Championships, winning as many as thirty-eight medals—including twenty-eight golds—between 1978 and 2005. From 1984 to 1993, Fischer was married to Jörg Schmidt, also a canoeing champion and winner of the silver medal in the C-1 1000 metre event at the 1988 Seoul Olympics. In fact, two more of her family members would later win medals in the same sport—her niece Fanny, winning a gold in the K-4 500 metre event for Germany at the 2008 Beijing Olympics; as well as her brother Frank, winning nine world championship medals from 1981 to 1986.

After retiring from canoeing, Fischer joined politics and ran for the Free Democratic Party in the European Parliament election in 1999. Though she did not win, Fischer continued to work as an ambassador of the sport and in 2004, she was recognized for her achievements by being voted the German 'Sportswoman of the Year'.

- Fischer's long Olympic reign in kayaking has given her the record for being both the youngest–at eighteen years–and the oldest–at forty-two years–Olympic champion in the event.

- Saint Innocent of Alaska is believed to be the Patron Saint of kayaking.

BJÖRN BORG

When you are at the top of your game, it takes the confidence of a legend to walk away from the spotlight. Amazingly, this is what Björn Borg dared to do. The Swedish tennis great shares the twentieth-century record for five successive Wimbledon singles championship titles with Roger Federer though Borg retired when he was only twenty-six. He left a lasting influence not only on how tennis would be played but also on the cultural hallmarks of the game.

Born in the Swedish capital of Stockholm on 6 June 1956, Björn Borg first held a tennis racquet when he was nine years old. By the time he turned fifteen, he was already on his country's Davis Cup team and even more incredibly, emerged the winner of both his singles matches. The next high point of Borg's game came in 1972 when he lifted the Wimbledon junior championship title and this was followed by other victories in Berlin, Barcelona and Miami.

After turning professional, Borg arrived at Wimbledon in 1973 amidst a wave of female fan frenzy. He won the title mere days before turning eighteen and then swept away the French Open shortly afterwards—becoming the then youngest winner at the Roland Garros centre court.

However, it was in 1976 that Borg began his dominance at Wimbledon where he would go on to win the singles championships five consecutive times. The last of these would come after a gruelling four-hour showdown with John McEnroe, and which was eventually decided by a marathon 34-point fourth-set tiebreaker. Indeed, this match would go on to be remembered as one of the epic encounters in the history of tennis.

It was not just at the Wimbledon grass courts that Borg proved his mettle. He won the French Open title for four consecutive years (1978–81) with six wins in total. In a span of merely seven years (1974–81), he swept away eleven major singles championships and was a five-time Grand Slam finalist. Between 1977 and 1981 too, he reigned as the world's No.1 player for a total of one hundred and nine weeks besides posting a record thirty-three-game winning streak in the Davis Cup play. Thus, by the time he retired at only twenty-six years of age, Borg was already a phenomenon with a staggering sixty-eight career titles in his pocket. There were a few half-hearted attempts at comebacks in 1991, 1992 and 1993, but eventually he would keep to his decision to call it quits.

Off the courts, Borg initially appeared to lead a whirlwind life. He went through two divorces and fathered a son out of wedlock. He was even hospitalized in 1991 because of a suspected accidental drug overdose, though he denied it later, clarifying it was brought about by food-poisoning. Eventually, Borg found stability in his life—he settled down to a fulfilling marriage in 2002 and had a second son.

Björn Borg, during the brief time of his reign on the tennis courts, exerted an unprecedented level of popularity. His two-handed backhand, top-spin-heavy ground strokes, wooden racquet and long blond hair kept in place with a headband, created a phenomenon that would certainly take a long time to match.

- Borg was nicknamed the 'Ice Man' for his cool temperament on the courts.
- He has his own clothing line, named 'Björn Borg', which is one of the most popular brands in Europe.

BOB MATHIAS

Bob Mathias was an American athlete who became the first winner of two successive Olympic gold medals in as tough an event as the decathlon. By the time he retired from the tracks, Mathias had pocketed an additional nine victories in nine competitions, four United States championships as well as three world records—all before turning twenty-two. After a brief stint in the armed forces and even on the silver screen, he went on to join politics and served a remarkable four terms in the United States Congress.

Born as Robert Bruce Mathias, the future decathlete had niggling health problems in his early childhood. However, guided by his doctor father, young Mathias soon gained physical strength. By the time he was competing in high school track and field events, he was already towering at six feet and two inches and 190 pounds. While Mathias's speciality was the shot-put and the discus, at the suggestion of his coach Virgil Jackson, he started training for the decathlon and in the summer after his high school graduation, qualified for the United States Olympic team that was going to London for the 1948 Olympics.

At the London Olympics, seventeen-year-old Mathias became the youngest winner of a track and field event when he won the gold at decathlon. But it was a hard-fought win, achieved under exceedingly difficult physical conditions such as heavy rain, fog and biting cold. After his return home, Mathias was personally welcomed by then President, Harry S. Truman. He also won the James E. Sullivan Award for America's outstanding amateur athlete.

Mathias successfully defended his Olympic gold four years later at Helsinki. Despite a pulled thigh muscle, his win at the 1952 Olympics made him the first athlete to win successive gold medals for decathlon in the history of the Games. However, the very same year, he shocked the world by announcing his retirement from sports.

Mathias then went on to graduate from Stanford University in 1953 with a Bachelor's degree in education and then served as an officer from 1954 to 1956 in the United States Marine Corps. After his return to civilian life, he was drawn to acting, appearing in TV series and even a movie inspired by his own achievements, titled *The Bob Mathias Story*.

In 1967, Mathias joined politics by becoming a Republican Senator from the Fresno area to the House of Representatives—a position that he continued to hold for four terms till 1974. In 2006, Mathias succumbed to a long fight with cancer—he was seventy-five.

With his youthful charm, clean image and quiet ambition, Mathias became a national sporting icon at just seventeen years of age when he won his first Olympic gold for decathlon. The repetition of his Olympics feat as well as his successive public life appointments, all contributed to his legacy of fair-mindedness and clean competitive spirit—all hallmarks of a true sportsperson.

- In an interview to the *Olympic Review* in 1975, Mathias recalled how he did not even know what decathlon was when his coach suggested that the young boy sign up for the event. Mathias apparently responded to Jackson's suggestion by saying, 'That's great, Coach; it sounds like fun. But just one question: What's a decathlon?'

- In Olympic decathlon, if an athlete fails to attempt any event, it leads to disqualification.

BOBBY JONES

Famous amateur American golfer Bobby Jones is best known as the first player to achieve the golf Grand Slam, when in 1930, he won all the four major tournaments of the time—the British Open, the US Open, and the British and US amateur championships—all in the same year. Jones came to be known as the first great American golfer for winning a whopping thirteen championships in those four annual tournaments, from 1923 through 1930—an achievement that would not be matched before 1973 by another American golfing great, Jack Nicklaus.

Born as Robert Tyre Jones Jr., on 17 March 1902, in Atlanta, Georgia, the future golfer was naturally blessed with the perfect swing, though during his childhood he is believed to have tried to copy Stewart Maiden, a Scottish golfer who was then the Atlanta Club golf professional. When he was only fourteen years old, Jones won his first US amateur championship at the Merion Cricket Club in Ardmore, Pennsylvania—a title that he would go on to sweep four more times. Besides this, Jones won the US Open four times, the British Open three times and one British amateur championship too.

The high point of Jones's career undoubtedly came in the year 1930 when he won the Grand Slam. Over a period of five months that year, he swept away the US Open, the British Open, and the US and British amateur championship titles—thus making history by becoming the first person to win all the four major tournaments of the American golf calendar.

Shortly after this feat, Jones retired from active golfing—he was just twenty-nine at the time. However, his interest in the sport continued and in 1934 he set up the Augusta National Golf Club. The same year, Jones was also among the major founders of a new tournament titled 'The Masters' which eventually came to replace the US amateur in the Grand Slam.

He was at the height of his career and had even defeated top pros of the time such as Walter Hagen and Gene Sarazen. However, it was only after his retirement from the game—when he started making films about golfing—that the sport brought him any revenues. For his contribution to golf, Jones received many honours, among which was the 'Freedom of the Burgh of St. Andrews' in 1958 in Scotland, which is famous as the home of the premier golf club of the world. With this award, Jones became the first American to be honoured thus; the last was Benjamin Franklin in 1759. By the time of his death in 1971, Jones was universally acknowledged as one of the most influential figures in the history of golf.

- A lawyer by profession, Jones never played golf to make money.
- As a child, Jones was often sick and unable to eat solid food till five years of age.

BOBBY MOORE

One of football's legendary players, Bobby Moore is best known for leading the English national team to its only World Cup win in 1966. A widely respected captain, thorough team player, defender par excellence and an exemplar of true sporting spirit, Bobby Moore was held in high esteem, both on and off the football field.

Born on 12 April 1941, in Barking, Essex, Moore was into sports since early childhood. However, he initially played cricket and even represented the Essex youth team. Eventually, Moore realized that his true passion lay in football and in 1956, signed up with the West Ham United (WHU) junior team. Two years later, he made his debut in the regular team, marking the beginning of an association that would see him representing WHU a whopping total of 544 times over the next sixteen years.

The highlight of Moore's football career was the 1966 World Cup where he led the national team against Germany in the finals and returned home with the championship title. The significance of this achievement can be gauged from the fact that this remains England's only win at the Fédération Internationale de Football Association (FIFA) World Cup, the holy grail of international football tournaments.

In 1970, Moore was chosen once again to captain the English team at Mexico, but the team was unable to defend its World Cup title. Even though Moore gave his all in the quarter-final match against Brazil, England lost. According to many sports commentators, Moore's game in this match superseded even his World Cup win. Not surprisingly, his hug with Pele after the 1970 quarter-final is considered to be one of the greatest visual moments of World Cup history.

During the course of his international career, Moore was awarded one hundred and eight caps for England which continued to be a record for an outfield player till David Beckham acquired his one-hundred-and-ninth cap in 2009. What makes Moore's achievement truly significant is that this was a time before substitutions were allowed and unlike modern caps, Moore played for the entire length of the match.

Moore was also famous for his long innings with his club WHU, which he captained for more than ten years, leading it to its 1964 Football Association Challenge Cup (also known as the FA Cup) win as well as the European Cup Winners' Cup trophy in 1965. From 1974 to 1977 however, he played for Fulham; interestingly, his last appearance in an FA Cup final, in 1975, was on the side of Fulham and against his old club, WHU. Later, he would also go abroad to appear in the United States soccer leagues before retiring from active playing in 1978. In February 1993, Moore succumbed to a long battle with cancer and was mourned not only by football fans in his home country but across the world. A superb defender and respected captain on the field, Moore left a rich legacy of fair play and integrity off it as well—today his bronze statue outside the Wembley Stadium entrance stands as a testimony to one of the giants of the sport of football.

- Before arriving in Mexico for the 1970 World Cup, Moore was arrested by the Columbian police on charges of jewellery theft. Though Moore was later proclaimed innocent, it was typical of his professionalism to show no signs of the trauma of the arrest and imprisonment on his demeanour and his performance during the tournament.

- After retiring from football, Moore partly owned several pubs and bars across East London, the most successful of which was Mooro's.

- Football legend Pele called Moore the greatest player he had ever played against.

BORIS BECKER

In the course of his career, tennis player Boris Becker would eventually capture fifteen doubles and a staggering forty-nine singles titles, among which would feature five Grand Slam championships—remarkable achievements that would earn him a place in the International Tennis Hall of Fame in 2003.

Born at Leimen, near Heidelberg, which was part of then West Germany on 22 November 1967, Boris Becker first learnt to play tennis at the Blau-Weiss Tennisklub or the hometown tennis club built under the supervision of his architect father. By the age of eight, Becker was already playing competitively and in 1984, he made his debut in professional tennis.

When the very next year, Becker reached the final of the Wimbledon men's singles, he was just seventeen years and seven months old. By defeating then eighth-seeded Kevin Curran in four sets in the finals, Becker set several records, such as becoming the first non-seeded player as well as the youngest to win the Wimbledon trophy. His record as the youngest player to win a Grand Slam title would not be broken for another four years till 1989 when a four-month-younger Michael Chang would go on to win the French Open men's singles title. In 1991, Becker won his fifth major title by beating Czech powerhouse, Ivan Lendl, in the Australian Open and with this, for the first time in his career, attained the No.1 overall ranking.

Along with the professional circuit, Becker was also a regular presence in Davis Cup tournaments where he represented Germany and even led his team to victory in 1988 and 1989; in fact there was a time in his career when Becker won twenty-two straight Davis Cup singles matches. In 1992, he won the gold medal at the Barcelona Olympic Games along with partner Michael Stich.

Becker retired from tennis in 1999 after losing to Patrick Rafter in the fourth round of Wimbledon—this seemed fitting too, since Becker shot to stardom because of his unique prowess on the famed grass courts of the All-England Club. His lightning-speed serve, electric volleys on the courts as well as unheard-of sums in prize money, all contributed to making Becker the pin-up boy of world pro tennis. This kind of adulation often brought complications too, among which were reports of tax evasion as well as an affair leading to a messy divorce.

However, in recent times, Becker has channelled his competitive urge into business and now has his own sporting equipment as well as apparel brands. Currently, he lives with his family in Schwyz, Switzerland. In 2003, Boris Becker was inducted into the International Hall of Fame for his many achievements in the sport.

- Tennis whiz Boris Becker is best remembered for being the youngest winner of the Wimbledon men's title when he lifted the Cup as a mere seventeen-year-old in 1985.

- In the 1987 Davis Cup, Becker defeated John McEnroe in one of the longest matches in tennis history, lasting six hours and twenty-two minutes.

- Becker famously refused to back Unified Germany's bid to host the 2000 Olympics, fearing a revival of nationalist extremism.

BRIAN LARA

Brian Lara is one of cricket's most famous names and widely considered as one of the greatest batsmen in the history of the sport. Even decades after his retirement, the West Indian cricket icon continues to hold the record for the highest number of runs within a single inning—both in international Test as well as first-class cricket.

Born on 2 May 1969 into a large family of eleven siblings, Brian Lara was nevertheless lucky to get an opportunity for good cricket coaching from early childhood. His stellar performance with the willow made Lara a champion in the schoolboys' league because of which he was selected in the Trinidad national under-16 team when he was only fourteen years old. This was soon followed by his entry to the West Indies under-19 national team. In the 1987 West Indies Youth Championship, Lara captained the Trinidad and Tobago team which eventually won the finals on the strength of his 116 runs.

Lara's first-class debut came in January 1988 when he played against Leeward Islands in the Red Stripe Cup. Two years later, in 1990, Lara found a place on the West Indian national team and the same year, he made his international debut—both in Test and One Day International (ODI)—against Pakistan in Lahore.

However, it would be another four years before Lara would stun the world of cricket with his batting prowess. In 1994, he smashed a stupendous 375 runs against England, thus overtaking

Sir Garfield Sobers's 365 runs (not out), in a single inning against Pakistan. Also in the same year, Lara set another record when he scored a staggering 501 runs (not out) for his English county team, Warwickshire. Ten years later, Lara would again deliver a master's knock with his 400 runs (not out), against England. With this total, he beat the 380 runs scored by Australian batsman Matthew Hayden in 2003. In the process, he become the first player in the history of cricket to reclaim a batting record in international Test.

Despite Lara's many breathtaking knocks, the West Indian team would go through a poor phase in the 1990s. The incongruity between the team's losses and Lara's own personal batting success as well as his lacklustre captaincy of the West Indian cricket squad, would cast a shadow on an otherwise glittering cricketing career. Indeed, by the time Lara finally retired, he held the record for the highest aggregate runs in Test cricket.

Lara's retirement in April 2007 from international cricket brought the curtains down on a truly glorious era of West Indian cricket. Lara's exit—for the first time since the country got Test status in 1928—left the team without any cricket stalwart.

As one of the most successful batsmen of all times, Brian Lara has been feted the world over. For two years in a row—1994 and 1995—he was honoured with the 'Wisden Leading Cricketer in the World' award and in 2012, he was inducted to the International Cricket Council's Hall of Fame. He is also one of just three cricketers—the others being Sir Garfield Sobers and Shane Warne—to have been awarded the prestigious BBC 'Overseas Sports Personality of the Year'. Lara has thus ensured that his name would be included with those of Sir Garfied Sobers, Sir Don Bradman, Clive Lloyd and Sir Viv Richards, as among the iconic batsmen of international cricket.

- Brian Lara was popularly known as the 'The Prince of Port of Spain'.
- Lara counts Indian cricket icon Sachin Tendulkar as one of his closest friends.

CARL LEWIS

American sprinter Carl Lewis is best remembered for ruling track and field events in the last decades of the twentieth century. He competed in four Olympic Games in the course of which he won as many as nine gold medals, the most famous being his haul of four at the 1984 Los Angeles Olympics.

Born as Frederick Carlton Lewis on 1 July 1961, in Birmingham, Alabama, the future athlete grew up in a family that nurtured both arts and sports. Just as he was taken to music concerts and plays, the young Carl was also encouraged to take part in athletic events in the local town club. Before long, he was on a winning spree which helped him to get a place at the University of Houston in 1980. The very next year he became the only person—after the legendary Jesse Owens—in NCAA history to win the 100 metres and long jump at the college championships. Consequently, he was named the top US amateur athlete in 1981.

Despite his stellar performance at home, Lewis could not compete in the 1980 Olympics because, in that year, the United States government led a sixty-five-nation boycott of the Moscow Olympics to protest against the Soviet invasion of Afghanistan in 1979. In 1984 however, Lewis swept away all competition at the Los Angeles Olympics, finishing the Games with four gold medals.

Lewis's Olympic career spanned three more Games, including the 1988 event in Seoul, the 1992 meet in Barcelona and the 1996 Games in Atlanta. At the end of this prominent career, he had garnered as many as nine medals, including a final gold in the long jump at Atlanta—an achievement that catapulted him back to the No.1 ranking in the event. It was a remarkable feat, considering fifteen years had passed since he had first claimed the top spot.

Even outside the Olympics, Lewis's performance was equally stellar and he finished the World Championships with eight career gold medals. In 1997, he took part in the 4×100 metres relay at the Berlin Grand Prix after which he finally retired from active sports.

In recognition of his long, illustrious track and field career, Lewis was named the 'Olympian of the Century' by *Sports Illustrated* in 1999 as well as the 'Sportsman of the Century' by the International Olympic Committee (IOC).

- The highlight of the 1984 Olympics was Lewis's 100 metre sprint in which he wowed audiences by racing ahead of the nearest competitor by a record 8 metres.

- Carl Lewis is a strict vegan.

- The first gold medal Lewis got for winning a 100 metre sprint is buried with his father.

COLIN MEADS

Hailing from the small island country of New Zealand, Colin Meads is widely considered as one of the most famous names in the Rugby Union and perhaps the best lock player in the history of the sport. Between 1957 and 1971, he played one hundred and thirty three games for the club, All Blacks, as well as fifty-five Test matches for the New Zealand national team. Known as much for his imposing height as for his physical tenacity, Meads came to be a revered icon of the country's sporting culture.

Born as Colin Earl Meads on 3 June 1936 in Cambridge, he grew up on a farm in King Country, where he probably developed his passion for the active life. In 1955, he made his debut while playing for his home province of King Country. This would also be the team for which he would play for the rest of his provincial career—in all, comprising one hundred and thirty nine games.

However, Meads is better known for his association with the All Blacks, for whom he played for the first time in 1957 when the team was touring Australia. He continued to be on the All Blacks team till 1971 when they experienced their first series loss to British Lions. Following this, Meads played in two President's XV matches against the All Blacks, even leading his side to victory in the match played at Athletic Park.

For the New Zealand national team, Meads played fifty-five international Test matches and even captained his side in 1971. Nicknamed 'Pinetree' because of his towering stature, Meads was equally known for the uncompromising physicality of his game. He would crush opponents just as he would himself continue to play even when injured. This was the time when substitution was not allowed and the game demanded a much greater level of physical tenacity from its players than today.

In another incident characteristic of his single-minded passion for the sport, Meads breached the South African boycott in 1986 when he led the rebel New Zealand Cavaliers to the African nation. He was completely against sports playing second fiddle to politics and hence, broke the ban which had been placed on South Africa because of its policy of apartheid. Such was Meads's stature in New Zealand that he was soon brought back into the official fold and appointed Manager of the All Blacks for the 1995 World Cup.

Above all, there was no doubting Meads's devotion to the sport. Playing in the pre-professional era, he hardly made any money from the sport but what he gained was all-round respect. In 1999, Meads was named 'Player of the Century' by the New Zealand Rugby Football Union. Having already been awarded the 'Member of the British Empire' in 1971, in 2000 he was honoured as the 'Distinguished Companion of the New Zealand Order of Merit' for services to the sport of rugby and the community at large.

- While playing against Eastern Transvaal during the 1970 South Africa tour, Meads broke his arm but continued playing till the end.

- On being addressed as Sir Colin, he once said, 'Just Colin; none of that other rubbish.'

DALEY THOMPSON

Daley Thompson is synonymous with the sport of decathlon. He is the winner of two Olympic gold medals in the event—in 1980 and 1984—and of every decathlon competition he entered from 1978 till 1988.

Born as Francis Ayodele Thompson in London on 30 July 1958, the future athlete was the son of a Nigerian father and a Scottish mother.

Decathlon is a challenging event which comprises of ten track and field components, including long jump, shot-put, high jump, hurdles, discus throw, pole vault, javelin throw as well as 100, 400 and 1,500 metre runs in separate events. Indeed, if an athlete withdraws from even a single event, he is out of the entire competition. Despite such tough conditions, Thompson made his debut in the event when he was only sixteen years old when he signed up at the Welsh Open decathlon in June 1975. He not only won the event but, with a score of 6,685 points, also set a British junior record in decathlon. Though he qualified for the 1976 British Olympic team, Thompson's performance at Montreal was disheartening as he finished 18th in the event. Two years later however, he improved to the extent of finishing 2nd at the 1978 European Championships.

1980 ushered in the best phase of Thompson's career as he first set a world record for decathlon in May and then swept away the gold in the event at the Moscow Olympics. Two years later, he set world records twice and seized the 1st position next year too, in the 1983 world championships. Thompson's gold rush continued in the Los Angeles Olympics too, and his 1984 gold helped him tie the record for successive Olympic gold medals in decathlon with American athlete Bob Mathias who had won gold medals in the 1948 and 1952 Olympics. At the Los Angeles Olympics, there was some consternation for Thompson when his total of 8,797 points fell just 1 point short of the world record but next year, with the adjustment of the scoring tables for the decathlon, his Olympic point total was changed to 8,847, which then made him a world-record holder.

The Los Angeles Olympics actually proved to be Thompson's last successful Olympics, as in Seoul, he injured himself and was out of the competition. However, his colourful persona and frequent anti-establishment stance made him popular with the public at large and after his exit from the tracks, Thompson had a successful career with a TV talk show on sports and as a businessman after he launched in his own gym, Daley Fitness, in London.

- Thompson's father gave him the African name Ayodele which was later shortened to Dele, and then to Daley—the name which the world would recognize as one of the most famous decathlon athletes ever. His original name, Ayodele, means 'joy comes home'.

- Thompson appeared as one of the polystyrene heads on the sets of the TV show, *Blockbusters*.

DAVID BECKHAM

British football star David Beckham is one of the rare sports personalities who enjoy a rock star status as much off, as on, the field. Apart from playing for the English national team in the 1998 FIFA World Cup, Beckham has been associated with various clubs, most famously Manchester United (ManU) but also Real Madrid and the L.A. Galaxy.

Born on 2 May 1975, in Leytonstone, London, to Ned Beckham, an appliance mechanic and Sandra Beckham, a hair stylist, David was the second among three siblings. He grew up in a family that was not only passionate about football but ardent supporters of the famed English football club ManU. Thus, no one was much surprised when young David started playing football as early as eight years old. Just three years later, he won the coveted Bobby Charlton Soccer School's national skills competition—a feat which brought him to the notice of ManU selectors. Beckham was soon signed up for the youth division of the club and by sixteen, was part of its training division. At eighteen, he formally joined the club and in 1995, made his debut as a full-time ManU starter.

By 1997, Beckham had scored enough goals to be awarded the title of the Professional Footballers' Association 'Young Player of the Year' and by the time the English national team arrived in France for the 1998 FIFA World Cup, his name was one of the biggest draws of the tournament. However, neither did England win nor did Beckham shine on the field. But his club career did rise to dizzying heights. In 1999, his captaincy helped ManU win the Premier League title, as the FA Cup as well as the Champions League title.

With the World Cup fame once again eluding Beckham, even his ties with ManU appeared to be strained and in 2003, he moved to Real Madrid. Just as football fans across Europe were getting used to the change in affiliation, Beckham dropped a bombshell by announcing his decision to cross the Atlantic in 2007 to play for L.A. Galaxy as part of a whopping $250-million, five-year deal. Many speculated that in part at least, the move was driven to boost the Hollywood prospects of his pop-star-turned-actress wife, Victoria. Beckham's arrival in the United States heralded a whole new chapter for the American Major League Soccer as just within forty hours of the deal being announced, the Galaxy sold more than 5,000 season tickets. Unfortunately, the move across the Atlantic did not add much to Beckham's football glory and in 2013, despite winning a title with French club Paris Saint-Germain, he announced his retirement from active football.

Beckham, however, has been a winner with all his commercial ventures. Leveraging his celebrity status and wife Victoria's fashion brand, the football star has several lucrative endorsement deals in his kitty and has launched his own apparel brand with the result that today, David Beckham is among the most financially successful sportspersons of the world.

Beckham is an inspiration to budding footballers across the world and his success underlines the importance of following one's passion. In fact, in a 2007 interview to the American lifestyle magazine, *W*, Beckham recalled how, when being quizzed in school on what he wanted to become when he was older, he would inevitably reply 'a footballer' only to be asked again, 'No, what do you really want to do, for a job?'

'But that was the only thing I ever wanted to do', insists Beckham in the interview, giving his readers, fans and all sports lovers a lesson in never letting go of one's dream.

- In 2001, Beckam's last-minute free kick against Greece enabled England to qualify for the 2002 World Cup.
- Beckam has ornithophobia (fear of birds) as well as ataxophobia (fear of untidiness).

DHYAN CHAND

Dhyan Chand was an Indian field hockey player who won three Olympic gold medals—in 1928, 1932 and 1936—for his country. During the course of his career, he is believed to have scored more than four hundred goals and is justifiably revered all over the world as the first international star of field hockey.

Born on 29 August 1905, in the famous Indian pilgrim centre, Allahabad, Dhyan Chand spent most of his childhood moving from one town to another as part of an army family, before his father finally settled in the central Indian town of Jhansi. In keeping with the tradition of the British Indian Army of those times, Chand too, joined his father's regiment where he was introduced to hockey by Subedar-Major Bhole Tiwari.

From 1922 to 1926, Dhyan Chand mostly played in the army hockey tournaments but soon, he demonstrated his talent at the first Inter-Provincial (National) Hockey tournament that was held in 1925 to put together a team for the 1928 Olympic Games. The Olympic finals in Amsterdam did not begin well for India as three of its best players were suffering from health problems and Dhyan Chand himself was unwell. However, the Indian team gave it all and beat the home side to win India's first Olympic gold medal. With a stupendous total of 14 goals from five matches, Dhyan Chand turned out to be the top scorer of the tournament. His magical footwork and ability to conjure up goals made Dhyan Chand internationally famous as the 'The Wizard'.

Four years later in Los Angeles, India not only defended its Olympic gold medal but once again defeated the home team in the finals by a stupendous winning margin of 24–1, thus setting a world record at that time. India's success to a great extent was due to Dhyan Chand and his brother Roop Singh—now nicknamed 'The Hockey Twins'—who, between them, had scored 25 out of the total Indian 35 goals in the Olympic tournament.

For the third time in a row, the Indian hockey players were pitted against the home team at the Olympic finals—this time at Berlin in 1936. Despite a shaky start, the Indians found their rhythm in the second half and led by Dhyan Chand's three goals, they eventually beat Germany 7–1 to win their third gold medal.

Dhyan Chand continued to play internationally till 1948 and after retiring, became the Chief Hockey Coach of the National Institute of Sports, Patiala. Unfortunately, his last days were spent in financial difficulties and he died on 3 December 1979.

Along with many formal honours—such as the Padma Bhushan in 1956, renaming of the National Stadium in New Delhi as the Dhyan Chand Stadium in 2002 as well as the declaration of his birthday to be celebrated as National Sports Day in India—the legendary hockey star brought fame and international respect to the sport. Dhyan Chand became its first star and played a crucial role in winning India its three Olympic gold medals, which, till date, remain the only ones the country has won in a team sport.

- Incidentally, the final hockey match of the 1936 Olympic Games was held on 15 August–a day on which, eleven years later, India would attain its independence from colonial Britain.

- There is a popular story that during a game in Germany, Adolf Hitler was so fascinated by Dhyan Chand's hockey skills and sportsmanship that he was willing to make him a Marshal in the German army.

- Vienna, in Austria, has a statue of Dhyan Chand with four hands and four hockey sticks.

DIEGO MARADONA

Considered one of the greatest footballers in the history of the game, Argentine star Diego Maradona is renowned for his footwork and ability to score, despite daunting defence. Maradona led the Argentine national team to World Cup glory in 1986 besides enabling club teams to win championships in Spain, Italy and his home country.

Born on 30 October 1960, in Villa Fiorito, a province of Buenos Aires, Maradona grew up in a large family with seven siblings. Having received a football as a present on his third birthday, Maradona soon displayed his genius for the game. When he was just ten years of age, he started playing for Los Cebollitas, a boys' team which was a part of one of the biggest clubs in the country, Argentinos Juniors. Even before turning sixteen, Maradona was chosen for the senior team of the club, thus marking his professional debut in 1976. When he joined the Argentine national football team four months later, he became the youngest player to do so. In 1979, Maradona led Argentina's under-20 national team to junior world cup championship.

As a part of the regular national team, Maradona played for Argentina in the 1982, 1986, 1990 and 1994 World Cups. It was in the 1986 championship held in Mexico where Maradona displayed his awe-inspiring control of the ball and ensured that his team seized the championship. Additionally, Maradona's flair with the ball also played a role in Argentina's victory in the South

American championships of 1987 and 1989.

Among the clubs that Maradona played for were Boca Juniors, FC Barcelona and SS Napoli, each of whom would go on to win championship titles at various levels. With him on the team, Boca Juniors won the 1981 championship, FC Barcelona lifted the Spanish Cup in 1983, while SS Napoli swept the league title and cup in 1987 besides attaining the league title again, three years later in 1990.

In the 1986 quarter-final match with England, his stellar goal, after dribbling the ball from midfield past an army of defenders, has gone down as among the finest goals in football history. However, Maradona's career was not without its share of controversies as he was twice suspended from playing—once for cocaine possession and the other time, for testing positive for the drug, ephedrine, because of which he had to exit the 1994 World Cup mid-tournament. Despite his retirement as an active player, he has remained in touch with the game and is currently the manager of the United Arab Emirate club, Al Fujairah SC.

Maradona's popularity the world over owes as much to his wizardry with the ball as to his man-of-the-people image. This is especially in relation to his humble origins as well as his association with SS Napoli, which he steered to victory against other wealthier European clubs. With his boyish good looks, passion for the game and superb ball control, Diego Maradona will continue to figure among the football legends of all times.

- The 1986 FIFA quarter-final match against England witnessed Maradona's infamous 'Hand of God' goal, in which he scored with his hand but was allowed since the referee mistakenly thought it was a header.

- In 2005, Maradona started hosting a talk show on Argentine TV and brought Pele as his very first guest.

DON BRADMAN

Cricket legend Sir Donald Bradman is still considered the greatest batsman in the history of the sport. His Test batting average is yet to be matched even after more than fifty years since he retired. Apart from this, he went on to become a successful captain and an astute selector—the Australian embodiment of sporting passion.

Born on 27 August 1908, in New South Wales, Bradman was so passionate about cricket from his childhood that he often practised on his own—reportedly with a golf bat or a cricket stump for a bat. He made his international debut during the 1928–29 Ashes season. Though Australia lost the series, Bradman's twin centuries announced to the world that a batting wizard had arrived.

Bradman returned from the 1930 Ashes tour of England with a staggering 2,960 runs, including ten centuries. After a brief period of ill health, Bradman regained his form and during the 1938 tour of England, he played twenty-six innings and racked up a stupendous total of thirteen centuries.

Military duty in the Second World War worsened Bradman's nagging health problems but he returned to the pitch in the mid-1940s. In March 1948, Bradman captained the Australian side during an eigth-month tour of England in which the former won every match. Consequently, the team became famous as 'The Invincibles'—the greatest Australian side in history. The same year, he also played his final Test at The Oval against England but shocked the crowd by getting out for a duck. Just four more runs would have given him an average of 100 but even then, his actual of 99.94 remains unmatched to this day. In the fifty-two Tests that Bradman played during his career, he hammered out twenty-nine centuries and posted a whopping total of 6,996 runs. After retiring, Bradman became an administrator and selector, paving the way for a new generation of Australian cricketers.

By the time of his death on 25 February 2001, Sir Donald Bradman had passed into the history of cricket as an embodiment of personal dignity and batting genius.

- Interestingly, as a young adult, Bradman got so interested in tennis that for two years, he gave up cricket.

- The threat posed by Bradman's batting was perceived by England to be so extreme that the latter devised a new dangerous pace bowling technique that became infamous as 'Bodyline'.

EDDY MERCKX

While the sheer magnitude of victories may not be the sole factor on the basis of which someone can be adjudged the greatest professional cyclist in history, Belgian cyclist Eddy Merckx's record is nonetheless commendable. Over the course of a thirteen-year-long career, he entered hundreds of races and racked up a stupendous total of four hundred and seventy six wins; fifty-four of them were in just one year—1971.

Born as Edouard Louis Joseph Merckx on 17 June 1945, in the small Belgian town of Meenzel-Kiezegem, the future cyclist never had any doubts as to where his passion lay. From the time that Merckx was gifted a cycle at the age of four and through all the years at school, he would never lose sight of his dream of becoming a professional cyclist.

Thus, when in 1962, Merckx asked his parents if he could drop out of school to pursue his passion for cycling full-time, it didn't take them long to agree. The same year, he entered fifty-five races as an amateur and won twenty-three, among which would be Belgium's national championship. In 1964, Merckx entered the Amateur World Championship Road Race and won that as well.

The following year, Merckx turned professional and even before his twenty-first birthday, he won the Milan–San Remo cycle race in Italy in 1966. For more than a decade henceforth, Merckx would come to dominate the world of professional cycling. In 1968, he won the Paris–Roubaix race and the next year saw him claiming the first of his five Tour de France titles. With the 1969 Tour de France win, Merckx set a record for acing every part of the gruelling race—for the fastest mountain climb, he was awarded the Polka-Dot Jersey; for scoring the maximum points, he got the Green Jersey; and for overall victory in the race, Merckx was honoured with the Yellow Jersey.

Though the later part of 1969 was clouded by a severe accident, Merckx was soon back on a winning spree. In 1970, 1972 and 1974, he won the Giro d'Italia, and in 1973, he achieved victory at the Vuelta d'España. In fact, in 1974, he became only one of two cyclists—the other being Stephen Roche much later in 1987—to have attained the feat of winning all three prestigious competitions of professional cycling—the Giro d'Italia, Tour de France, and World Championship Road Race.

Yet another high point of Merckx's career came in 1972 when he set a new record for the greatest distance travelled by a cyclist in one hour—49.4 kilometres, or 30.7 miles—but what made this a truly remarkable feat was that it came about in the high altitudes of Mexico City.

In 1978, diminished by recurring injuries, Merckx finally announced his retirement from professional cycling. However, his association with the sport continued as he later started his own business in high-end cycles and took up TV commentary as well. He even coached the Belgian national cycling team for eleven years, from 1985 to 1996.

Even in these times of superior technology and extreme bicycles, Merckx's competitive spirit and physical endurance remain legendary in the world of professional cycling.

- Due to his voracious appetite for entering competitions and winning them, Merckx was nicknamed 'The Cannibal'.
- Merckx was awarded the title of 'Baron' in 1996; this title is for life, but cannot be inherited.

EDWIN MOSES

One of the most famous names from track and field history, American athlete Edwin Moses dominated the 400 metre hurdles in the 1970s and '80s. He not only claimed the gold medal in the 400 metre hurdles over two consecutive Olympic Games, but won a staggering one hundred and twenty two consecutive races in the same event over the course of a decade.

Edwin Moses was born on 31 August 1955, in Dayton, Ohio, into a family of educators. With both parents involved in academics, young Moses always took his studies seriously. Even while studying at the Fairview High School, he was part of both the basketball and football teams, besides appearing on the track and gymnastics floor.

It was only after Moses enrolled into the Morehouse College in Atlanta, Georgia, on an academic scholarship, that he began taking his sporting abilities seriously. Despite the non-availability of proper training area, Moses signed up for the college track team and began competing in the 110-metre-high hurdles, 400 metres and 4×100 relays, before finally deciding to focus on 400 metre hurdles for the approaching 1976 Olympics.

At Montreal, Moses stunned the world, not only by seizing the gold medal in the 400 metre hurdles but even setting a world record of finishing at 47.63 seconds. After returning home, he shifted his attention to studies but not before he had reduced his own time to 47.45 seconds and won the World Championship title.

In 1978, Moses graduated from college with a bachelor's degree in physics, thus displaying an enviable balance between academic and sporting pursuits which is the hallmark of the ultimate achiever.

After that however, the track claimed all his attention and soon Moses proved to the world that his 1976 Olympic gold was no fluke. Though he missed out on the 1980 Moscow Olympics because of the American boycott, the same year, he set a new world-record time of 47.13 seconds. In 1983 again, he broke the record with a career-best blitz of 47.02 seconds.

In the 1984 Los Angeles Olympics, Moses once again won a gold medal, thus becoming only the second athlete in history to win consecutive Olympic gold medals in the 400 metre hurdles. At Seoul four years later, though Moses's performance was his best in an Olympics final, it was not enough to win him a gold and he returned with a bronze medal.

Eventually, he directed his efforts at fostering a healthier sporting environment. In 1983, he had already joined the Athletics Congress whose goal was to discourage the use of anabolic steroids in his sport and in 1992, he was nominated to the IOC Medical Commission. Eventually, Moses became the head of the United States Olympic Committee's Substance Abuse, Research and Education Committee, where he played a major role in formulating anti-drug policies in sports.

- After bidding the track adieu, Moses took up the relatively unknown sport of bobsledding and even won a bronze medal in the 1990 World Cup race.
- He has also been the chairman of the prestigious Laureus World Sports Academy.

EMIL ZÁTOPEK

Czech athlete Emil Zátopek is widely regarded as one of the greatest runners of all times. He is still the only athlete to have won the prestigious 'Triple Crown' comprising of the 10,000 metres, 5,000 metres and marathon in a single Olympic Games tournament. Apart from this stupendous achievement, Zátopek's legacy also includes the method of interval training in distance running which many athletes follow till today.

Born on 19 October 1922, in the small Czech town of Kopřivnice, Zátopek grew up in a large family of eight children to a carpenter father and a homemaker mother. In order to share the family's financial burden, young Zátopek took up a job in a shoe factory when he was just sixteen. However, the employment would prove providential as in 1941, a race sponsored by the shoe factory through the town of Zlín, saw Zátopek compete for the first time. Though he came second in this race, word of his running ability began getting around and soon he was encouraged to compete in a 3,000 metre run that would become his debut official race. After he finished this race, his trainer, and the appreciation that followed, compelled Zátopek to seriously consider running as a profession.

But this was the time of the Second World War and with Russia's invasion of Czechoslovakia, Zátopek found himself in the army. After the end of the World War in 1945, things began to look up again for Europe's athletes and in 1948, Zátopek arrived in London to compete at the Olympic Games. He not only won a gold medal in the 10,000 metre race but bagged the second place in the 5,000 metre race as well. Three years later, on 29 September 1951, Zátopek finished a 20 kilometre race in less than an hour—the first person in the world to do so—and in the process, broke four world records in just one race.

It was the 1952 Helsinki Olympics that would mark the pinnacle of Zátopek's running career. Here he bagged all the three long distance races—the 10,000 metre, the 5,000 metre as well as the marathon—thus sweeping the Triple Crown of the Olympic races during a single meet. In fact, at Helsinki, Zátopek also set a new Olympic world record as he slashed the previous record for the 10,000 metre race by 43 seconds.

In Melbourne for the 1956 Olympics, Zátopek—recuperating from a recent surgery—opted out of the 5,000 metre and 10,000 metre races to focus solely on the marathon. Unfortunately, he came a distant 6th and after competing in a few more shorter races in the following years, he finally retired from competitive running but not before he had pioneered the interval training method which alternates short bursts of high speed with longer periods of low-speed running.

The turbulent politics behind the Iron Curtain[*] brought about a sharp downturn in Zátopek's fortunes during the 1970s and '80s. Eventually, with the liberation of Czechoslovakia from Communist rule in 1990, Zátopek was reinstated to the position of dignity and honour that he retained till his demise in 2000.

---

[*]The Iron Curtain is a term for the metaphorical boundary drawn by Soviet Russia to isolate itself and its allied European countries from contact with the liberal democracies of the West.

- Zátopek's wife, Dana Zátopková, was also a participant in the Helsinki Olympics. Just before she began competing in the javelin throw, Zátopek loaned her his second gold medal which she put in her bag for good luck. Incredibly, Dana not only won the event with the first throw but set a new Olympic record too.

- About his passion for running, Zátopek once said, 'A runner must run with dreams in his heart, not money in his pocket.'

FANNY BLANKERS-KOEN

One of the pioneers of women's track and field history, Dutch athlete Fanny Blankers-Koen became the first—and even almost seventy years after the achievement, the only—female track and field athlete to win four gold medals at a single Olympics. So versatile were her athletic talents that she set world records in as many as seven events.

Born as Francina Elsje Koen on 26 April 1918, in Baarn, in the Netherlands, the future athlete grew up in a family that encouraged sports. Thus, right from early childhood, she could swim, skate and play tennis. When Koen was fourteen, she began to focus on specialized training upon her father's advice who recognized her special aptitude for track and field.

In 1935, Koen entered her first official competition when she ran a 200 metre race in Groningen. Though she did not do well in that, she soon found her rhythm and by next month, had become the Dutch national champion in the 800 metre race. The following year, Koen left for Berlin to take part in the 1936 Olympics where she competed in the 4×100 metre relay. Though she did not return with a medal, Koen continued her steady rise to the top of women's athletics. In 1938, she matched the world record at a 100 yard dash in Amsterdam and over the next few years, she set world records in the 80 metre hurdles, high jump as well as long jump. This was also a time of personal happiness for Koen as she married her coach and pillar of support,

Jan Blankers, in 1940.

Support was something that Koen would need substantially as she arrived in London for the 1948 Olympics. On one hand, there was the pressure to better her previous Olympics tally while on the other, she had to encounter the sexist opinions of people who thought that as a wife and mother, she had no business running in the Olympics. Added to this was the institutional discrimination according to which women at that time could participate only in three individual Olympic events. In fact at one time, the stress got so intense that she broke down and told her husband that she was withdrawing from all competitions. Eventually though, Koen would return from London with four gold medals won for 80 metre hurdles, a 100 metre sprint, a 200 metre race and the 4×100 metre relay.

After rules for pentathlon underwent modification in 1951, Koen became not just the first woman but the first athlete to set a modern record for the event with a whopping 4,692 points. In order to honour her contribution to the history of athletics and especially of the pioneering role she played in the visibility of female athletes, Koen was named the 'Top Female Athlete of the Twentieth Century' by the International Association of Athletics Federations (IAAF) in 1999. Like a true legend, she remained modest about her achievements and once said, 'All I've done is run fast. I don't see why people should make much fuss about that.'

- In the 4×100 metre relay at the 1948 Olympics, Koen was the last to receive the baton but overtook the lead just before the finishing line.

- Koen was nicknamed 'The Flying Housewife' since, by the time she was running in 1948, she was a mother of two kids and pregnant with her third child.

GARETH EDWARDS

Welsh national Gareth Edwards is one of the world's foremost names in Rugby Union football. In a career spanning over a decade, he has played both for the national team of Wales as well as for the British Lions club.

Born on 12 July 1947, in Gwaun-Cae-Gurwen, Wales, into a miner's family, Edwards was keen on sports right from his childhood. At school, apart from rugby, he played soccer and also participated in athletics and gymnastics. This helped young Edwards to secure a scholarship to the prestigious Millfield School in Somerset, England, which was especially famous for honing sporting talent.

In 1967, at just nineteen years of age, Edwards made his international debut when he got selected to the Welsh national team to play against France at the Parc des Princes in Paris. Though Wales lost that match 20–14, it announced the arrival of a star on the horizon of the rugby-playing world.

The very next year, Edwards—at just twenty—led the Welsh team against Scotland and with it, set a record as the youngest Rugby Union captain in his country. From 1967 to 1978, Edwards played fifty-three Test matches for the Welsh national team, of which thirteen were played as its captain. He also played ten Tests for the club, British Lions, which later came to be known as the British and Irish Lions. Over this period, he scored 88 points with twenty tries in the process. Edwards's consistent success led him to be named 'Player of the Year' in Wales in 1969 and the BBC 'Wales Sports Personality of the Year' in 1974.

Edwards played his final international match in 1978 at Cardiff. Just like his debut, he and his team were once again pitted against France but the difference was that this time Edwards and his mates won 16–7, thus marking the perfect finish to a legendary career. For his services to the Rugby Union football in particular and sports in general, Edwards was made a Knight Bachelor in May 2015.

- Gareth Edwards is best remembered for winning the Five Nations Championship a whopping eleven times.
- He had a legendary partnership with Barry John, epitomized in the quote: 'Just throw it; I will catch it'.

GARFIELD SOBERS

While there have been scintillating batsmen and ruthless bowlers in the game of cricket, a rare player stands tall for his all-round achievements. Famous as one of the greatest all-rounders of cricket, Sir Garfield Sobers is as much remembered for his dignified behaviour on the field as for an exemplary life off it, thus standing as the true knight of what used to be known as the 'gentleman's game'.

Born on 28 July 1936, in Bridgetown, Barbados, young Garry was a cricket enthusiast like the majority of the community. He studied at Bay Primary School in Barbados where he got the opportunity to hone his cricketing skills by playing in teams from other clubs and schools.

When only sixteen, Sobers made his first-class cricket debut against the touring Indian team in January 1953. The first time he played an international match was during the 1953–54 season, when he bowled for the West Indies national team against England.

Sobers went on to have a twenty-year-old international Test career during which he led the West Indies national team on thirty-nine occasions as the captain. Apart from playing for his country, he also played for, and captained, the Nottinghamshire English county team from 1968 to 1974.

Sobers displayed immense skill as both a left-handed batsman and left-handed bowler. Over a two decade-plus Test career, he amassed 8,032 runs which included a staggering twenty-six centuries as well. Among his greatest batting moments were his score of 365-not-out for West Indies against Pakistan in 1958 (which was overtaken only after thirty-six years, in 1994), as well as his stupendous six 6s off six balls of an over in Glamorgan, in a county cricket game where the last 6 hit by Sobers landed far beyond the stands. The greatest recognition of Sobers's expertise perhaps came from the Master himself when his score of 254 in the match played by Rest of the World XI against Australia was appreciated by Sir Don Bradman as the best innings ever made in cricket.

At the same time, Sobers was an extremely successful bowler which is demonstrated by his tally of 235 wickets at an average of 24. More importantly, his bowling repertoire was varied, ranging from medium pace to left-arm spin. Additionally he could field competently in any position but got especially good results when placed close to the wicket.

Above all, Sobers lived to the true spirit of cricket with his innate sense of fair play and gentlemanly conduct, both on and off the field. For example, during the 1967–68 English tour of West Indies, Sobers declared a Test, enabling the visitors to win the match and the series. Again, in the second match of the 1970–71 series when Indian captain Ajit Wadeker insisted that he had won the toss in a crucial match, Sobers graciously conceded. In recognition for his contribution to cricket, Garfield Sobers received a knighthood in 1975 and was nominated by *Wisden* as among the 'Five Greatest Cricketers of the Twentieth Century'.

- Interestingly, Sobers was born with an extra finger on both hands, which, according to his autobiography, *Garry Sobers: My Autobiography*, he got rid of himself—the first wrenched off by a piece of catgut and the other taken off by a sharp knife!

- Sobers had a fantastic 1960-61 tour of Australia in which he scored 430 runs, took 15 wickets and even one catch—a feat that prompted Don Bradman to invite Sobers to play for South Australia.

GREG LOUGANIS

Greg Louganis is an American diver who has won thirteen world championships as well as two Olympic gold medals. In 1982, at the Guayaquil World Championships, he became the first diver to be awarded the perfect 10 in the history of the sport.

Greg was an adopted child in the Louganis family. Unfortunately, his adoptive father was often physically abusive at home and this compounded young Greg's problems who was already being picked on by kids at school for his mixed-race origins.

However, young Louganis found solace in physical activities such as dance and gymnastics. Upon experimenting with his moves in the pool, the boy discovered his aptitude for diving and began competing when he was only nine. Two years later, at the 1971 Junior Olympics, he scored a perfect 10 in diving and emerged a national champion as a mere eleven-year-old.

Louganis made his Olympic debut in 1976 at Montreal where he won the silver medal in the 10 metre platform diving event. He could not take part in the next Games because of the American boycott of the 1980 Moscow Olympics. But Louganis proved that it was worth the long wait to the next Olympics, when in 1984, he swept the men's 3 metre springboard as well as the 10 metre platform events at Los Angeles. With these two gold medals, he reached the pinnacle of his diving career.

But despite his remarkable Olympic performance, Louganis

officially retired the following year, mainly because he had discovered before the Seoul Games that he was HIV positive. Writing about his life in his bestselling autobiography, *Breaking the Surface*, Louganis revealed the truth about his homosexuality as well as his HIV-positive status. In later TV interviews, he also discussed his lifelong struggles with substance abuse and depression.

Having seen so many highs and lows, Louganis has since taken on the role of a motivational speaker as well as an activist for dyslexic children and gay rights. His success is yet another reminder of the need to treat everyone fairly, irrespective of gender, race, sexuality, class and other such man-made discriminatory factors. In 2013, Louganis made a place for himself in the California Sports Hall of Fame and in 2015, he was chosen to be the torchbearer for the Special Olympics World Games in Los Angeles.

- In 1988 at the Seoul Olympics, Louganis suffered an accident at the 3 metre springboard preliminaries and had to leave the pool. But incredibly, he came back sutured just half an hour later and not only went on to win the gold medal for the event but for the 10 metre platform as well.

- Louganis graduated with a major in theatre and minor in dance from the University of California in 1983.

- After retirement, Louganis became an agility trainer for his show dogs in Malibu, California.

HAILE GEBRSELASSIE

Ethiopian athlete Haile Gebrselassie is widely recognized as the greatest distance runner of modern sports history. This is not only because of the number of 10,000 metre championship titles under his belt—including two Olympic gold medals and four World Championships—but also because of the sheer range of his winning distances, from 1,500 metres to the marathon.

Gebrselassie was born on 18 April 1973, in Asella, in the Ethiopian province of Arsi. He grew up in humble circumstances and experienced the lack of basic schooling near his home. Eventually, Gebrselassie's gift for running long distances began to be known beyond his school and soon he was taking part in official competitions. During these years, Gebrselassie looked up to another running star from his own country—Abebe Bikila— who had returned with the Olympic gold medal in 1960 and had since been an inspiration to many Ethiopians.

Gebrselassie's first international victory was the Junior World title for 5,000 metres and 10,000 metres that he won in 1992. The very next year, he moved up to the senior competitions and promptly seized the World Champion title for the 10,000 metre race—the first of his four world championship titles which he would go on to win in the same event for another three consecutive times—in 1995, 1997 and 1999. In fact, in 1995, Gebrselassie set a new world record in both the 5,000 metre as well as 10,000 metre events.

The successful decade of the 1990s included Gebrselassie's Olympic performance as well. In 1996, at the Atlanta Olympics, he won the gold medal for the 10,000 metre race which he successfully defended four years later in Sydney.

Eventually, Gebrselassie began focusing on marathons. In 2001, he won the IAAF half marathon and the next year, he finished third at the full marathon in London. In 2007, he set a new world record for marathon timings when he finished the Berlin marathon in an amazing 2 hours 4 minutes and 26 seconds. Incredibly, he would go on to lower even this record the next year and at the same event by finishing the 2008 Berlin marathon in 2 hours 3 minutes and 59 seconds. Even while approaching his fortieth birthday, Gebrselassie amazed the world by winning the 2013 Vienna half marathon in a time of 1 hour 1 minute and 14 seconds. After competing in the 2015 Great Manchester Run, he finally announced his retirement from competitive running.

Gebrselassie is well known for his simple but regular training regimen. In recent years, he has expressed a desire to enter Ethiopian politics in order to leverage his international fame towards working for the development of his country.

- The early practice of running 10 kilometre every day to attend a school situated far away ensured that Gebrselassie acquired extreme endurance.

- Some sports analysts have commented that Gebrselassie's running posture of a bent left arm looks as though he is still holding his schoolbooks.

HEATHER McKAY

Australian sporting icon Heather McKay is today respected as a pioneer of women's squash and the most famous female player in the history of the sport. Apart from squash, she was also a talented player of other sports such as field hockey and racquetball.

Born in Queanbeyan, New South Wales, on 31 July 1941, McKay grew up with a love of sports and outdoors. She started playing competitive squash in 1960 and the same year, she lost the quarter-final of the New South Wales Championship to Yvonne West. However, this would be one of only two losses in her two-decade-plus career of competitive squash. The second defeat would come in 1962 at the finals of the Scottish Open.

However, from 1962 till 1981, McKay would never again lose even a single match of squash. In 1962, she won the British Open for the first time—a feat she would go on to repeat over the next fifteen years. When the first women's World Open officially began in 1979, McKay won the championship easily in England—a feat that she repeated in 1979.

Heather McKay also played squash at the amateur level, and from 1960 to 1973, she claimed the Australian Amateur Championship title for fourteen straight years.

McKay's dominance of the world of women's squash during the decades of 1960s and '70s was unquestioned. She wrote about her experiences and achievements in a book titled *Heather McKay's Complete Book of Squash,* which was published in 1979.

Even after retiring from competitive squash, she continued to be associated with the sport—first in the capacity of the Australian Institute of Sport's Squash Division coach and then as one of the founder members of the Women's International Squash Players Association Hall of Fame and, not surprisingly, McKay was the first player to be inducted into it. Next year, she was the recipient of one of the highest sporting honours of her country when she was awarded the Australian Sports Medal in 2000. In recognition of her stellar career and services to sports, she had already been honoured as Member of the Order of Australia in 1979 as well as a Member of the Order of the British Empire (Civil) a decade before that, in 1969.

- McKay's sporting genius can be gauged from the fact that even during her best years as a squash player, she was successful in other sports as well. In 1967 and 1971, she was a member of the Australian women's hockey team, while in racquetball, she won one American Amateur Racquetball Championship title, three American Professional Racquetball Championship titles and five Canadian Racquetball Championship titles.

- McKay has only lost two matches in her entire career.

HICHAM EL GUERROUJ

Hicham El Guerrouj is a Moroccan middle distance runner, best known for being the first to set world records for the mile and 1,500 metres races, both indoors as well as outdoors. He is a four-time winner of the 1,500 metres World Championship besides having three Olympic medals under his belt—of which two are gold, won for 1,500 metres and 5,000 metres at Athens in 2004.

Born on 14 September 1974, in Berkane, Morocco, Guerrouj discovered his passion for running only in his teens. He also sought inspiration from the achievements of fellow Moroccan athlete, Said Aouita, who returned to the country with a gold medal in the 5,000 metres from the 1984 Los Angeles Olympics.

1995 was the year of Guerrouj's first major athletic achievement when he claimed the title for the 1,500 metres Indoor World Champion. The title of the 1,500 metres Outdoor World Champion for the same year, however, went to Algerian distance runner Noureddine Morceli who would prove to be Guerrouj's chief opponent in the rise to the top of the world rankings.

1996 saw Guerrouj's first Olympic appearance at Atlanta where he faced his old rival, Morceli, at the 1,500 metres outdoor race. Unfortunately, just before 430 metres of the finishing line, Guerrouj crashed into Morceli and fell to the ground. Though he returned to the race, Guerrouj would be the last to finish. This would, however, be one of only three times, over a nine-year-long career, that Guerrouj would lose among all the eighty-six finals that he appeared for the 1,500 metres and the mile.

Though the Olympic medal had eluded him, El Guerrouj proved his mettle in the World Championships. In 1997, with a new time of 3 minutes and 48 seconds, he broke the indoor 1,500 metres world record and then went on to set a new bar for the indoor mile too with his time of 3 minutes and 48.45 seconds. The year 1999 saw El Guerrouj keeping up the winning streak. With a new time of 3 minutes and 43.13 seconds, he established a world record in the mile and even claimed the world championship title for the 1,500 metres outdoor event.

Eventually, in 2000, El Guerrouj won an Olympic medal at the Sydney Games, though he had to settle for the silver in the 1,500 metres race which was won by Kenyan runner Noah Ngeny. However, El Guerrouj's domination of the World Championships continued and in 2001 as well as 2003, he racked up a total of thirty-two wins.

Finally, in 2004, El Guerrouj managed to realize his Olympic dream when he won not one, but two gold medals at Athens—in the 1,500 metre as well as 5,000 metre races.

Two years after his Olympic high, El Guerrouj retired from competitive racing. Currently, he remains associated with sports initiatives such as the Monaco-based Peace and Sport as well as Champions of Peace, which are committed to promoting harmony among communities in different parts of the world.

- In recognition of his achievements, El Guerrouj was nominated as IAAF 'World Athlete of the Year' in 2001, 2002 and 2003, thus becoming the first recipient of the prestigious award over consecutive years.

- El Guerrouj dedicated his Athens victory to his infant daughter Hiba as well as Morocco's King, Mohammed VI.

IAN BOTHAM

English cricketer Ian Botham is widely regarded as one of the finest all-rounders in the history of Test cricket. In England he is especially remembered for his spectacular knock of 149-not-out which took the English team from certain defeat to a miraculous win at the 1981 Ashes Test at Headingly.

Born as Ian Terence Botham on 24 November 1955, in Heswall, Cheshire, the future all-rounder revealed his sporting potential right from childhood. He was not only good at cricket but at football too—even going on to play on the Scunthorpe United team for a while. However, it was cricket where Botham's heart lay. By the age of eighteen he had already made his first-class debut when in 1974, he played for Somerset. His association with the club would continue for twelve seasons before coming to an end in 1986 when Botham resigned to protest the unceremonious exit of his West Indian friends, Sir Vivian Richards and Joel Garner, from the Somerset team.

Botham made his international debut in 1977 and the very next year, while playing against Pakistan at the Lords, he became the first player to score a century and take 8 wickets in a Test. In 1979, he set another record for becoming the fastest all-rounder to boast of a Test tally of 1,000 runs as well as 100 wickets—incredibly enough, he achieved the goal in merely twenty-one matches.

However, it was his 149-not-out at the 1981 Ashes in Headingly that would go down in the annals of Test cricket as one of the top knocks to turn around not just a match but an entire series. It was largely due to the psychological boost from Botham's batting and bowling in the last two matches of the series, that England was able to recover from their footing from the first three tests and lift the Ashes Cup at Old Trafford.

In 1982, Botham set the record for the fastest Test double of 2,000 runs and 200 wickets which came out of just forty-two matches. For the 1986–87 tour of Australia, Botham once again spearheaded the English recovery with his century in the first match at Brisbane as well as his haul of 5 wickets in the first innings at Melbourne—both of which went a long way to help England win the series.

Botham's larger-than-life presence on the cricket field was often mirrored in his controversial conduct off the field too. He often got into confrontation with other cricketers and officials and was once even suspended for smoking cannabis. Apart from being decorated with the 'Order of British Empire' in 1992, Botham has been honoured with the BBC 'Sports Personality Lifetime Achievement Award' in 2004.

- After retiring from cricket, Botham got busy with TV commentary.
- His initiatives, such as Charity Walks, have been greatly successful in raising money for welfare projects.

IAN THORPE

Nicknamed 'Thorpedo' for his shooting speed in water, Australian swimmer Ian Thorpe has won five Olympics gold medals—the most by any individual athlete in the history of his country—besides being the youngest to win a World Aquatics Championship title.

Born on 13 October 1982, Thorpe grew up in a sports-loving family in a Sydney suburb known as Milperra. By the age of eight, Thorpe was swimming competitively and when he was only fourteen, he became the youngest swimmer to qualify for the Australian national team.

The first high point of Thorpe's international career came in 1998. Aided by his body length of six-feet five-inches and incredible swimming speed, he not only won the 200 metre and 400 metre freestyle events at the world championships but also broke a 400 metre world record with his time of 4 minutes 46.29 seconds. He was just fifteen years old and thus, also set the record for being the youngest World Swimming Champion.

Following his 1998 world championship records, Thorpe became the toast of Australian media and was already billed as an Olympic favourite at Sydney in 2000. Performing on his home ground, Thorpe made no mistake and practically swept away most of the high-profile swimming events with a haul of four medals—a gold each for 400 metre freestyle, 4×200 metre freestyle relay and 4×100 metre freestyle relay besides one silver medal in the 200 metre freestyle.

Thorpe's gold rush continued the following year as well. At the 2001 World Aquatics Championships, he set individual world records in the 200 metre freestyle, the 400 metre freestyle as well as the 800 metre, besides being part of the winning 4×200 metre freestyle relay team, which set its own world record. By the end of the meet, Thorpe had racked up a total of six gold medals which helped him to win the title of 'Best Male Performer' and his country to be declared as the champion team.

At the 2003 World Aquatics Championships, Thorpe won another three gold medals thus proving his domination in the world of competitive swimming. At the Athens Olympic Games held next year, he emerged victorious in the 200 metre and 400 metre freestyle events besides coming 2nd in the 4×200 metre freestyle relay and 3rd in the 100 metre freestyle. His total haul from the 2004 Olympics included two gold, one silver and one bronze.

Eventually, the stress of such highly competitive meets began to take its toll and Thorpe decided to take a year off from his swimming career. Despite preparing for the 2006 Commonwealth Games, he couldn't compete because of an illness. In November 2006, Thorpe stunned the world of sports by announcing his retirement—he was just twenty-four years old! Though he tried to make a comeback in the 2012 London Olympics, he was unable to qualify.

Outside the pool, Thorpe has kept himself busy, working for various charitable causes. In 2000, he founded the Ian Thorpe's Fountain for Youth, which works for children with disabilities besides raising research funds for paediatric diseases.

- Incredibly, when Thorpe first tried swimming, he turned out to be allergic to the chlorine in the pool but eventually overcame the condition as he learnt to swim with his head outside the pool.

- The size of his feet is an incredible 17!

- Thorpe narrowly avoided death in the 9/11 attack on the World Trade Center. He had gone to see the towers, but returned to his hotel upon realizing that he had forgotten his camera. In was in that interim period, that the incident occurred.

IMRAN KHAN

Perhaps the most widely recognized Pakistani cricket player, Imran Khan enjoyed as much popularity for his cricketing skills as for his personal charisma. His greatest moment of glory came in 1992 when he led Pakistan to lift the World Cup. Eventually, he joined politics and founded his own national party, the Pakistan Tehreek-e-Insaf.

Imran Khan was born on 25 November 1952, in an affluent family of Lahore. Though he was always on the school and college cricket teams during his student days in Pakistan and the UK, it was while studying at Oxford University that Khan played his first international Test cricket match in 1971. However, it was only after his graduation from Oxford University that he accepted a permanent position on the national team.

Imran Khan's all-round abilities were clear from the very beginning—his ability to hit substantial knocks when required as well as fast bowling, ensured a wide fan base beyond national borders. Even more remarkable were his leadership skills on the cricket field. It was largely due to his astute guidance as a captain that Pakistan went on to win the 1992 World Cup. By the time Khan announced his retirement from active cricket next year, he had under his belt, a total of 3,807 runs and 362 wickets in Test matches.

At the time of his retirement, Khan was undoubtedly the most recognized Pakistani face on the world stage and he soon decided to leverage his celebrity status for public purposes. In 1994, he founded a specialized cancer hospital in Lahore which was named Shaukat Khanum Memorial Cancer Hospital after his mother, whom Khan had lost to cancer in 1985.

Khan's personal charisma has also been responsible for successive romantic attachments. His 1995 Paris wedding to Jewish-born British heiress Jemima Goldsmith, raised eyebrows in both countries. The marriage lasted nine years after which Khan married British-Pakistani newsreader Reham Khan in a private nikah ceremony in January 2015. However, the same year, the couple announced their decision to file for divorce. Khan's third marriage was to a lady called Bushra Maneka in 2018. Currently, he remains busy with politics and has emerged as an important player on the national stage.

- Khan's former wife Jemima is the daughter of UK billionaire Sir James Goldsmith.
- Though Tehreek-e-Insaf was slow to garner votes, it now leads the coalition government in the north-western Pakistani province of Khyber Pakhtunkhwa.

JACK NICKLAUS

One among the most famous names in the history of professional golf is that of the American, Jack Nicklaus. In a twenty-five-year-long career, he won eighteen major championships, among which six were Masters. Both feats went on to set world records in professional golf.

Born to Ohio-based Charlie and Helene Nicklaus on 21 January 1940, in Columbus, Jack was introduced to the sport when he was only ten. The Columbus-based Scioto Country Club Juvenile Championship was his first tournament and there his amazing performance brought him to the notice of then club pro, Jack Grout. Grout became his first important coach whose influence paid off as Nicklaus won the Ohio Open as a mere sixteen-year-old. Next year, he claimed the International Jaycee Junior Golf Tournament championship title.

After finishing high school, Nicklaus enrolled into the Ohio State University and continued to play as an amateur. He won the United States amateur title in 1959 and the same year, he also married his college sweetheart Barbara Bash with whom he would go on to have five children. In 1961, Nicklaus won the Amateur title again, besides seizing the NCAA Championship. In November that same year Nicklaus turned professional.

Not surprisingly, Nicklaus won the US Open title the very next year. In 1963, he tasted his first victory at the Masters Tournament and the following year, he laid claim to the

PGA Championship title. Despite having many victories on the United States pro circuit, Nicklaus would have to wait till 1966 to win the prestigious British Open. This was also the time when he was repeatedly pitched against another golfing legend, Arnold Palmer, who enjoyed greater popularity among the audience.

The decade of the 1970s saw a change in Nicklaus's public persona as he became leaner and donned brighter colours on the greens. Also, at the same time, he began releasing books on golf in collaboration with long-time mentor Jack Grout and writer Ken Bowden. All these positive changes reflected in his game as well and he continued his winning spree. In 1973, he even got ahead of Bobby Jones's career record of ten major titles. Two years later, Nicklaus won both the Masters and the PGA Championship and in 1980, he seized the PGA title as well as the US Open. The last of his six Masters titles came in 1986. In this match, despite beginning the final round four strokes behind New Zealander Ross Norman, Nicklaus whipped up an unimaginable 6-under-30 back 9 to lift the trophy. At forty-six years of age, Nicklaus became the oldest golfer to win the Masters, just like twenty-three years ago, he had been the youngest to win the same title.

Nicklaus has won legions of fans because of his intense focus and all-round golfing skills. In November 2005, he was awarded the Presidential Medal of Freedom by then President, George W. Bush. Currently, he remains busy with various business interests which range from wine and apparel companies to his golf-course-designing firm titled Nicklaus Design.

- Jack Nicklaus has been nicknamed 'The Golden Bear' for his golden hair and stocky figure.
- He has been colour blind all his life.

JACKIE JOYNER-KERSEE

Jackie Joyner-Kersee is a former American athlete who is widely regarded as the pioneer of women's foray into multiple track and field events. Her tally of three gold, one silver and two bronze medals is a record that remains unbroken in women's Olympic track and field history.

Born on 3 March 1962, in East St. Louis, Illinois, to teenage parents, Jacqueline Joyner-Kersee grew up in difficult circumstances. Even then, with encouragement from her mother and an inborn determination, young Jackie was determined to excel both in studies and sports.

In 1980, Jackie joined the University of California, Los Angeles (UCLA) on a basketball scholarship. At this time, her potential was spotted by assistant track coach Bob Kersee, who insisted that Jackie train for the multi-event track. He even persuaded the university to change her scholarship from basketball to the heptathlon.

The new direction turned out to be the right one for Jackie. In the 1984 Olympics, held before a cheering home crowd, she won the silver medal in the heptathlon—missing the gold by a mere .06 seconds in the final event, the 800 metre run. In the same championships, her brother, Al, won a gold medal in the triple jump—becoming the first American sportsperson in eighty years to do so.

At the Moscow Goodwill Games next year, Jackie scored a

staggering 7,148 points in heptathlon and in the process, set a record for being the first woman to cross 7,000 points in this event. Only three weeks after this, she beat her own mark with a score of 7,158 points at the US Olympic Festival in Houston, Texas. In recognition of her achievements, Jackie was honoured with the James E. Sullivan Award and the Jesse Owens Award, in 1986. The year also brought personal happiness for her. In January, she tied the knot with Bob Kersee after which she began to be known as Jackie Joyner-Kersee.

In 1988, Jackie again won a gold medal in the heptathlon at the Seoul Olympics and with a score of 7,291, she established her fourth world record. Even more amazingly, she beat all competitors in long jump, thus not only becoming the first American woman to win an Olympic gold medal in long jump, but also the first athlete in sixty-four years to win both a single as well as multi-event gold medal.

Four years later, Jackie would not only go on to defend her heptathlon gold at the Barcelona Olympics but win a bronze medal in long jump too. Her final Olympic medal came in 1996, when she won the bronze medal in the long jump at Atlanta. Indeed, Jackie continues to hold the record for the maximum distance attained by an American athlete in long jump.

Jackie retired from track and field in 2001 and in 2007 she was awarded the 'Women in Sport' trophy by the IOC. Her real legacy, however, lay in the way she popularized the sport of heptathlon worldwide and paved the way for female track and field athletes to achieve heights as great as their male counterparts.

- According to family lore, the Joyner parents christened their oldest daughter after the then First Lady of United States, Jacqueline Kennedy, upon which one of her grandmothers even commented, 'Someday this girl will be the First Lady of something'.

- During the height of her athletic form, Jackie Joyner-Kersee had just 6 per cent body fat.

JAHANGIR KHAN

Pakistani squash player Jahangir Khan is widely regarded as the most famous player in the history of the sport. Among his incredible feats are winning the World Open six times as well as the British Open championship for a staggering ten consecutive times—from 1982 to 1991.

Born on 10 December 1963 into a family where squash was professionally played, Jahangir's entry into the sport was only expected. And yet he had to confront several challenges, in the form of ill health, before acquiring skill and fame as a squash player. After a couple of hernia operations, his father encouraged him to try out a few games and soon Jahangir proved his potential on the squash court. Even then, he was prevented by his country's selectors from entering the 1979 world championships in Australia. In response, Jahangir decided to compete in the World Amateur Individual Championship and returned with the title as well—aged just fifteen, he had already set his first world record as its youngest champion.

However, tragedy struck soon and in November the same year, Jahangir's elder brother Torsam, who was then one of the most promising international squash players, died suddenly of a heart attack during a match in Australia. The demise of his brother and mentor deeply affected Jahangir and for a time, he even thought of quitting the sport. Eventually though, he came to the realization that the best way to honour his late brother—who was among the first to believe in him—would be to keep playing.

In 1981, Khan won the World Open and at just seventeen, became the youngest winner of the title. Next year, he astounded the world of sports by winning the International Squash Players Association Championship without giving up even a single game—in fact, he would not lose another match for almost five and a half years till 1986 when Ross Norman would defeat him in the World Open finals in Toulouse, France.

Having cemented his reputation as the World Squash Champion in the first half of the 1980s, Khan decided to try his hand at the North American variant of hardball squash. Here too, he won twelve of the thirteen top-level hardball tournaments that he entered between 1983 and 1986. Having proved his superiority in both the softball and hardball versions of squash, Khan was regarded as the undisputed king of the sport at this time.

Jahangir Khan eventually met his match in fellow-countryman, Jansher Khan, and over the latter half of the 1980s, the world of squash would keenly watch both the giants of the sport contend for every game. The last time Jahangir Khan took home the World Open championship title would be in 1988, though he would keep up his winning streak at the British Open till 1991.

Jahangir Khan's long reign in the world of squash was in part due to his legendary physical stamina which fuelled his long rallies and eventually wore out opponents. Both in his country and around the world, Jahangir Khan has been feted with numerous awards among which have been the 'Sportsman of the Millennium' title bestowed by the Pakistani government. He was also conferred an honorary Doctorate of Philosophy by the London Metropolitan University. No wonder then that *Time* magazine wrote about the squash legend in 2006: 'If winning is everything, then Khan is the greatest.'

- 'Jahangir', in Persian, means conqueror and the squash legend has definitely earned that title.
- One of the most significant hurdles in Khan's life came in the form of ill health–as a child he had been advised by doctors against any form of strenuous physical activity.

JESSE OWENS

Widely revered as one of the fastest men in history, Jesse Owens attained worldwide fame overnight by winning four gold medals at the 1936 Olympic Games held in Berlin under the Nazi regime. His feat would not only go on to inspire generations of athletes after him but would especially act as a beacon of hope for people of African origin—proving that given equal opportunities, they could achieve anything.

Born as James Cleveland Owens on 12 September 1913, in Oakville, Alabama, the future athlete overcame childhood illnesses and economic difficulties to discover a passion for running at Fairmount Junior High School after the Owenses moved north to Cleveland in search of better economic opportunities.

It was while studying at East Technical High School that Owens started competing seriously. At the 1933 National High School Championship held in Chicago, he equalled the world record of 9.4 seconds in the 100 yard dash and clocked 24 feet and 9.5 inches in the long jump.

After joining Ohio State University, Owens went on to sweep the 1935 Big Ten with three new world records. At the NCAA Championships held the same year, he won four events, at the Amateur Athletic Union (AAU) Championships he won two events and at the Olympic trials, he won another three. The stage was set for Owens to work his magic at the Olympic Games next year.

The 1936 Olympic Games event was special for host Germany

as the then Nazi regime under Hitler was determined to prove its theory of Aryan racial superiority. However, Owens—an American of African origin—swept the athletic events by breaking two Olympic records and winning four gold medals. His success was the most definitive demolition of the Nazi theory of racial superiority and still serves to illustrate the fallacy of propagating any form of inequality based on unjustified factors.

However, distressed by the absence of government economic support after his return home, he took up commercial endorsements. This led to the United States Olympic Committee stripping him of his amateur status and banning him from further competitions. Owens was compelled, for a time, to even race against cars and horses to earn a living but in 1966, he had to file for bankruptcy.

Eventually, the United States government woke up to the seriousness of Owens's situation and he was made a United States goodwill ambassador. He soon found a new calling in motivational speaking which was part of the appointment's responsibilities. More significantly, Owens finally began receiving official recognition of his Olympic achievements. In 1976, he was honoured with the Presidential Medal of Freedom by then President Gerald Ford and also inducted into the Olympic Order for taking on racism during the 1936 Berlin Olympics. By the time Owens succumbed to lung cancer in 1980, his life and achievements had been firmly enshrined in history as a beacon of hope for generations of sportspersons to come.

- Soon after arriving in Cleveland, when young Owens was asked his name by a teacher at school, he replied 'JC'–as he was called in Alabama–but because of his thick Southern accent, the teacher understood it as 'Jesse' and the name stuck to him.

- Owens came back from the 1936 Olympics not only with medals and records but a life-long friendship with Luz Long. Despite the hyped-up rivalry between the two, the German athlete helped his main competitor by making a significant observation about Owens's run-up, thus helping the American to qualify for the long jump mains and eventually clinch the gold medal.

- In Berlin, Owens ran his gold-winning race in shoes handcrafted by the founder of Adidas.

JOE FRAZIER

Former American boxer Joe Frazier is regarded among the top heavyweight fighters of the world. In fact, he held the title of the World Heavyweight Boxing Champion for three years and is best remembered for giving Muhammad Ali a tough fight in the 1975 'Thrilla in Manila'.

Born on 12 January 1944, in Beaufort, South Carolina, into a humble family of sharecroppers, Frazier was the youngest of twelve children. Young Frazier had a difficult childhood and by the time he turned thirteen, he had already quit school. Things got worse and a couple of years later, he found himself struggling to get by on his own. Frazier soon moved to New York where his brother was working, but there too, he had trouble finding work. Despite all these challenges, Frazier continued to hold onto his dreams of becoming a boxer.

Eventually in 1961, Frazier got the chance to enter a boxing ring and soon the power of his knocks caught the attention of coach Yancey (Yank) Durham. With Durham's help, Frazier polished his technique and chiselled his famed left hook till he became the Middle Atlantic Golden Glove Champion—a title he retained for three years. Frazier's greatest success as an amateur came in 1964 when—despite being initially rejected by selectors—he went on to win the gold medal at the Tokyo Olympics.

Next year, Frazier turned pro and in 1968, he won the heavyweight championship title; a result that owed in part to

Muhammad Ali being banned for refusing to participate in the Vietnam War. When Ali returned to the ring in 1970, the stage was set for a showdown between the two heavyweight champions. Dubbed as the 'Fight of the Century', the highly anticipated match took place on 8 March 1971, at New York's Madison Square Garden. Frazier delivered a definitive victory and consequently became a boxing sensation overnight. However in 1975, he would unfortunately go on to lose their next most famous match—nicknamed 'Thrilla in Manila'—through a technical knockout.

Frazier announced his retirement from the ring in 1976. Though he did try to make a comeback in 1981, he soon realized it was time to pass the baton to the next generation as two of his eleven children went on to choose professional boxing as careers. In 2011, Frazier was diagnosed with liver cancer and on 7 November the same year, he succumbed to the disease.

- When Frazier first arrived in Philadelphia, he got a job at a slaughterhouse, where he would practise by punching the sides of beef hanging from hooks in a refrigerated room. This fact would later inspire actor Sylvester Stallone who would create such a scene in his 1976 iconic boxing film, *Rocky*.

- When he fought Muhammad Ali in the 'Thrilla in Manila', Frazier was already partially blind.

JOE MONTANA

One of the most famous names in professional American football, Joe Montana is regarded as the best quarterback in National Football League (NFL) history. He not only guided his team, the San Francisco 49ers, to four Super Bowl championship titles but retired with multiple career playoff records for touchdowns, completions, attempts as well as yards gained passing.

Born as Joseph Clifford Montana on 11 June 1956, in New Eagle, Pennsylvania, the future football star was competent at various sports right from his childhood. In fact, North Carolina State University offered him a basketball scholarship before he decided to join University of Notre Dame to play football. But with the University team already boasting of big names, it would be a while before he would see real action. The chance eventually came in 1977 when Montana led the Fighting Irish to the national championship title. Two years later, after helping his team defeat University of Houston at the Cotton Bowl, Montana was selected by San Francisco 49ers in the third round of the 1979 NFL draft.

Over the next fourteen seasons, Montana guided the 49ers to four Super Bowl victories—of which two came successively, in 1989 and 1990. In the process, he also set a record as the first player to be chosen three times for the Super Bowl 'Most Valuable Player' title. Among his most memorable performances during this period were touchdown passes—one in the final minutes of the 1981 National Football Conference Championship Game (which became famous as 'The Catch') and again a similar feat in the closing moments of the Super Bowl XXIII.

In 1993, Montana was traded to the Kansas City Chiefs with whom he played the last two seasons of his NFL career. Buoyed with their star quarterback, they won their first division title in twenty-two years besides playing their first Asian Football Confederation Championship Game in January 1994. The same year, Montana finally retired from active football and settled in his Northern California estate to pursue his lifelong interests of fine wines and country living.

During his playing years, Montana picked up several nicknames such as 'Cool Joe' for his incredible ability to remain calm under moments of extreme on-field pressure as well as the 'Comeback Kid' for an uncanny ability to turn around his team's fortunes and snatch victory from the proverbial jaws of defeat.

- The immense respect Montana commanded in the sport is clear from the fact that, in 2000–the first year of his eligibility–he was chosen into the Pro Football Hall of Fame.

- Montana owned an estate in Northern California wine country for many years.

KAREEM ABDUL-JABBAR

Iconic basketball player Kareem Abdul-Jabbar is one of the most successful names in the sport. In a career spanning two decades, the American was the winner of six National Basketball Association (NBA) titles and continues to hold the record for the maximum points in the history of the league. For the majority of his professional career, Jabbar played for the Los Angeles Lakers, helping it to claim the NBA championships as many as five times.

Born as Ferdinand Lewis Alcindor Jr. on 16 April 1947, in New York, the future basketball great gave evidence of his sporting genius as early as his teens. When he was still in high school, Alcindor led his team to a whopping seventy-one straight wins and three consecutive championships at the city level. At the same time, he set individual records for rebound and scoring among school players from New York City.

After his graduation, Alcindor enrolled in UCLA where he quickly established his prowess in the game. Under the guidance of John Wooden—one of the most influential coaches at that time—Alcindor led his college team to three national championships—in 1967, 1968 and 1969—for which he was feted as the tournament's 'Most Outstanding Player' by the NCAA for those years.

Not surprisingly then, Alcindor was lapped by Milwaukee Bucks in the first round of the 1969 NBA draft and the same year his performance in the professional league helped him to win the

'Rookie of the Year' award. In 1971, with his team winning the NBA championships, Alcindor received the first of his six 'Most Valuable Player' awards. The same year, he also converted to Islam and adopted the Arabic name, Kareem Abdul-Jabbar.

In 1975, Jabbar was traded to the Los Angeles Lakers. Driven by the basketball-centre's scintillating shooting skill, the Lakers lifted the NBA championship title five times—in 1980, 1982, 1985, 1987 and 1988. In fact, 1984 saw Jabbar set an individual milestone as well, when he beat Wilt Chamberlain's record of 31,419 points. Apart from his signature sky hook, Jabbar was also well known for a host of elegant post moves as well as his highly successful passes. By the time Jabbar retired after the 1988–89 season, he had won the 'Most Valuable Player' award six times besides setting records for maximum points (38,387) garnered, highest number of field goals (15,837) as well as most minutes played (57,446) in NBA history. In 1995, the Naismith Memorial Basketball Hall of Fame welcomed Jabbar in its fold and the next year, his name found a spot in the NBA list of its fifty greatest players in the history of the professional league.

Outside the basketball court, Jabbar had an interesting stint in TV and films, among which his comic role in the 1980 film *Airplane* became widely popular. He also wrote several books about his journey as a sportsperson of colour as well as the history of African American pioneers—achievements which finally culminated with the Presidential Medal of Freedom that Jabbar received in 2016 from then President, Barack Obama.

- Towering at seven-feet two-inches, Jabbar was always the tallest kid in class.
- Jabbar's offensive skill was such that Collegiate Basketball Rules Committee made dunking illegal in 1965, just before his signed up with UCLA. In fact, as soon as he graduated from college, dunking was again made legal.

KATIE LEDECKY

American swimming champion Katie Ledecky is currently among the fastest performers in the pool. Till 2017, she had won five Olympic gold medals and one silver medal, besides setting numerous world records in the sport.

Ledecky was born on 17 March 1997, in Washington, D.C., and right from her childhood, she displayed her skills in the water. She began swimming competitively when she was only six and by the time she was fifteen, she had already earned a place in the United States Olympic team—also setting a record as its youngest member—that was set to go to London in 2012. At the Olympics, Ledecky blazed forth in the pool, to win the gold with a time of 8 minutes 14.63 seconds and in the process, also broke the twenty-three-year-old American record set by Janet Evans.

Ledecky quickly proved that her Olympic glory was no fluke and she was the fastest female swimmer in the world now. At the 2013 Fédération Internationale de Natation (FINA), or International Swimming Federation, championships, she not only won four gold medals but also set world records in the 800 and 1,500 metre freestyle events. Next year, at the Pan Pacific Swimming Championships, Ledecky repeated her haul of four gold medals. By winning the 200, 400, 800 and 1,500 metre freestyle events at the 2015 FINA World Championships, she became the first woman to score multiple events at an internationally significant competition.

With her sights set firmly on the 2016 Olympics, Ledecky decided to delay college. But even before she arrived at Rio de Janeiro, Ledecky was already setting swimming records. Her eleventh world record came as she finished the 800 metre freestyle with a time of 8 minutes 6.68 seconds at the Arena Pro Swim Series. The same summer she also broke existing world records in the 400 and 1,500 metre freestyle events.

At the Rio Olympics, Ledecky dominated all freestyle events. She not only won a total of four gold and one silver medal, but also set world records in two races—the 400 as well as the 800 metre freestyles. It was typical of someone of her ability to win by wide margins.

Over her career, Ledecky has been feted with numerous awards, among which are the FINA 'Swimmer of the Year' in 2013, the United States Olympic Committee's (USOC's) 'Olympic Sports Woman of the Year' in 2016, as well as the Golden Goggles 'Female Athlete of the Year' on three occasions.

- At the 800 metre freestyles in Rio, Ledecky left behind her nearest competitor by a substantial 11 seconds.
- She volunteers with Bikes for the World, a non-profit that repairs old bicycles and sends them to budding cyclists in underprivileged places of the world.

KELLY SLATER

Kelly Slater is the world's most successful professional surfer. With as many as eleven world championship titles under his belt, he has dominated the sport for a period longer than any other competitive surfer.

Slater was born on 11 February 1972, at Cocoa Beach in the American state of Florida. Growing up around water—since his father kept a bait-and-tackle shop—he started surfing when he was just five. By 1984, he was already the winner of the first United States Surfing Championships title. This feat was followed by three straight titles which eventually brought him to the notice of surfing pioneer Matt Kechele. With the latter's guidance, Slater performed even better and at the Eastern Surfing Festival at Florida's Canaveral Pier, and went on to sweep away both the boys' division as well as the pro division titles, though he declined the prize money to retain his amateur status.

Upon turning eighteen, Slater turned pro and in 1990, he easily walked away from the Body Glove Surf Bout contest at Trestles with the $100,000 prize money. The next year, he made his world tour debut and managed to reach the 43rd place on the world rankings.

However, the year 1992 would turn out to be Slater's first year of full-fledged professional success and by the middle of the season, he was the top-ranked professional surfer. He also became the youngest surfer in the world to achieve the feat. After a brief dip in form in 1993, Slater was back to his winning ways with the world championship in 1994—the first of five straight such titles. In 1994 as well, he won the Pipeline Masters title, which he would go on to win consecutively till 1996 and again in 1999. Furthermore, Slater won the Grajagan Quiksilver Pro as well as Billabong Challenge title at Jeffreys Bay—all in 1995. Slater also bagged the Triple Crown title the same year—a feat that he would repeat three years later in 1998.

He returned to the waves in 1999 and went on to win the Pipeline Masters for the fourth time, while the next year, he seized the Gotcha Pro at Teahupo'o.

The new century saw the rise of a new opponent—Kauai's Andy Irons—on the pro surfing scene. In 2003 and 2004, Slater was bested by Irons. However, from 2005 onwards, the former was back in charge, first defeating Irons to lift his seventh world title and then in 2006, winning the tour championship as well. In 2008, Slater won his sixth Pipeline Masters trophy and in 2011, bagged his eleventh championship title—thus setting a record that remains unbroken till date. Two years later, he would win the Pipeline Masters title for the seventh time.

Widely acknowledged as the king of professional surfing, Kelly Slater has garnered more wins and prize money than any other competitor. More importantly though, he must receive the credit for transforming surfing from just another beachside recreation to a sport that can bring professional success and worldwide fame to the best talent on the waves.

- In 1998, Slater took a break from competitive surfing to pursue other interests such as music.

- Slater co-starred with former girlfriend Pamela Anderson in an episode of *Baywatch* in 1992.

LARISA LATYNINA

Iconic gymnast Larisa Latynina is best known for being the first woman in the history of Olympic Games to win nine gold medals. Even more incredibly, during the decade of her Olympics domination—from 1956 to 1964—she racked up a staggering tally of eighteen medals—a feat which remained unmatched for almost half a century until ace swimmer Michael Phelps surpassed it in 2016.

Life, however, was not so generous for Latynina in the beginning. Born as Larisa Semyonovna Dirii on 27 December 1934, in Kherson, Ukraine, the future gymnast grew up in a country that was newly incorporated into the Union of Soviet Socialist Republics (USSR). Along with the political dominance of Moscow, came the hardships of the Second World War and by the time she turned eleven, Larisa had lost both her parents.

However, because of the Soviet system of public education, Larisa's talent in gymnastic exercises was spotted early and she began to receive systematic training. The coaching helped and just as a sixteen-year-old, she won the national schools gymnastics championships. Though she did not make much of a mark in Rome at the 1954 World Gymnastics Championships, she did find some happiness in her personal life around this time. While at Kiev to attend the Physical Training College, she met Ivan Latynina, a fellow student, and soon married him.

Now competing as Larisa Latynina, she set her sights on the

1956 Olympics and sure enough, she, along with her teammates swept the gymnastic events at Melbourne. This marked the beginning of Soviet domination in international women's gymnastics which would continue for another half a century. Latynina herself returned from Melbourne with six medals, including three individual gold medals, one team gold medal, and one silver and one bronze medal.

Latynina continued her stellar performances in the European Championships as well. She won every event in 1957, and in 1958, she repeated the feat except for the vault. The birth of her daughter compelled Latynina to stay away from the 1959 European Championships but in the meantime, she was getting ready for Rome.

The 1960 Olympic Games saw Latynina reach the peak of her sporting career. She won three gold medals, respectively, in the floor exercise, all-round category as well as in team competition. For balance beam and uneven bars, she won two silver medals, while the vault brought her the bronze.

By the time the 1964 Olympics came around, Latynina was already thirty—an age when most gymnasts, whether male or female, are usually past their prime. However, that Latynina still had a lot more to give to the world of sports was evident in Tokyo where she excelled in team competition and the floor exercise, thus winning two gold medals. For the individual all-around and vault, she won silver and her performance in the balance beam and uneven bars, garnered her two bronze medals as well.

Though at the 1965 European Championships, Latynina managed to win four silver and a bronze medal, the next year, she finished 11th at the world championships, and realized it was time to officially retire. This would also signal her transition from active competition to coaching and under her expert guidance, a new generation of star gymnasts such as Natasha Kuchinskaya, Olga Korbut and Lyudmila Turishcheva, brought fame to the Soviet Union.

Latynina continues to be remembered for her signature style that combined ethereal grace with athletic skill. Her success not only heralded the long phase of Soviet domination in women's gymnastics but also marked her as a pioneer of women's presence in the Olympic Games.

- When eleven years old, Latynina took up ballet but moved to gymnastics when the dance studio closed a year later.
- When Michael Phelps broke her record for maximum Olympic gold medals, Latynina was at the stadium to personally cheer for him.

LEANDER PAES

Indian tennis star Leander Paes is best known for his two-decade-plus stint on the tennis courts which includes eight doubles and ten mixed-doubles Grand Slam titles. The year 2016 marked his seventh Olympic appearance—a feat rarely matched even by the international stalwarts of the game.

Leander Paes was born on 17 June 1973 in the eastern metropolis of the country, Kolkata (then called Calcutta). His mother hailed from the same city, though his father was Goan by birth. Both his parents were skilled sportspersons. Leander's father had been a mid-fielder in the Indian field hockey team that had won the bronze medal at the 1972 Munich Olympics while his mother had led the Indian basketball team in the Asian basketball championship of 1980. Therefore, it came as no surprise when young Leander exhibited an inclination for sports. In order to hone his budding talent, his parents enrolled him at the Amritraj Tennis Academy in 1985 based in Chennai (then called Madras).

In the same year, he joined the Indian Davis Cup team after which he turned professional in 1991. The next year, he reached the quarter-finals of the doubles event with Ramesh Krishnan at the 1992 Barcelona Olympics.

Paes's moment of highest Olympic glory came in 1996 when he defeated Fernando Meligeni to win the bronze medal at Atlanta. With this, he became the only Indian tennis player to have won a medal in the Olympic Games, besides bringing India its first individual Olympic medal in more than four decades. Before Paes, wrestler K.D. Jadhav had won the bronze medal at the 1952 Helsinki Olympics.

However, it is in the doubles matches that Paes proved his longevity as a tennis player. In 1994, he began partnering with fellow Indian Mahesh Bhupathi and the two went on to win six Association of Tennis Professionals (ATP) doubles titles out of the eight tournament finals they reached in 1997 and 1998. In 1999, the pair won the doubles events in the Wimbledon as well as the French Open, besides reaching the finals of the US Open and Australian Open. All of these achievements helped the duo ascend the heights of the doubles ATP rankings the same year.

However, differences cropped up between Paes and Bhupathi, though they would team up now and then—even going on to win the 2001 French Open doubles for the second time. Paes later began to pair up with others, most often Czech players. In 2006 and 2009, he won five more Grand Slam titles with various doubles partners, thus bringing his tally to eight, while in mixed-doubles, he has won a staggering ten Grand Slam championships till 2016. There is no doubt that Leander Paes has proven himself one of the most successful doubles and mixed-doubles tennis players in the history of the sport. More importantly, his long career has given Indian tennis a significant presence on the world map, thus inspiring later generations of players, such as Sania Mirza and other youngsters, to take up the sport.

- Paes catapulted to international fame when in 1990, he won the Wimbledon Junior title and was ranked No. 1 in the Junior World League.

- In 2012, Paes appeared in a Bollywood movie titled *Rajdhani Express*.

LEE CHONG WEI

Malaysian badminton player Lee Chong Wei is the most successful Olympic athlete of the country whose three silver Olympic medals have led him to be accorded the status of a national hero. He is also the only Malaysian badminton player who has been ranked No.1 in the world for over a year.

Born on 21 October 1982, in Bagan Serai, Perak, Lee Chong Wei began to play badminton from the age of eleven. Though he initially trained under a local coach, soon his talent was spotted by famous Malaysian player Misbun Sidek who took young Wei under his wings. The rigorous training under Sidek paid off and when he was just seventeen years old, Wei was drafted into the Malaysian national squad.

Wei's international career was slow to take off. In 2003, he reached the finals of the Malaysian Open but was defeated by China's Chen Hong. However, 2004 proved to be a better year since Wei not only swept the Chinese Taipei Open and the Malaysia Open but also qualified for the 2004 Olympic Games. At Athens though, he was again defeated by Hong in the second round.

The 2008 Olympics proved to be better since at Beijing, Wei reached the badminton singles finals though he was overwhelmed by Lin Dan's sheer brilliance on the court. Four years later, Wei defended his silver medal at the 2012 London Olympics despite having suffered an ankle injury earlier that year. In the 2016

Olympics, Wei defeated his long-time rival, Lin Dan, in the semi-finals but the gold medal still eluded the Malaysian star as he lost to Chen Long in the finals. Nevertheless, Wei earned his third straight Olympic silver, thus establishing himself as the only Malaysian sportsperson to have won the maximum number of Olympic medals.

Wei however, continued to ace other international badminton tournaments. He won the gold medal thrice in the Commonwealth Games and twice in the Asia Championships besides winning the Badminton World Federation (BWF) World Super Series finals four times, BWF World Super Series premier twelve times and the BWF World Super Series, a whopping twenty-nine times. Apart from these, he continued his silver run at the world championships three times and once at the Asian Games as well.

In recognition of his long contribution to Malaysian sports, Wei was accorded the revered title of 'Datuk' and was praised as a national hero in 2008 by the country's then prime minister, Datuk Seri Najib Tun Razak. Later in 2012, Wei also penned his biography titled *Dare to be a Champion* which, not surprisingly, turned out to be a bestseller in his country.

- Wei was initially interested in basketball. However, when his mother objected to it because of the searing heat outdoors, he began to take badminton more seriously.

- The title of 'Datuk' is limited to eight hundred living persons and comes with a lifetime pension of $1,161 a month.

LIN DAN

Widely considered the greatest singles badminton player, Lin Dan is a winner of two Olympic gold medals, five world championship titles as well as six All England Open Championships titles. The Chinese sportstar has the distinction of being the first and till 2017, the only player to complete the Super Grand Slam of badminton which includes the nine most coveted titles in the sport—namely, the Olympic Games, World Cup, BWF World Championships, Thomas Cup, Masters Finals, Sudirman Cup, All England Open, Super Series, Asian Games, as well as the Asia Championships. Nicknamed 'Super Dan', he complements his electrifying moves on the court with an aggressive image which have made him an inordinately popular sporting icon for the current generation. Also, he is the only badminton player to have successfully defended an Olympic gold in singles.

Dan was born in Longyan, in Fujian, China, on 14 October 1983. When he was only five years old, he began playing badminton. Eight years later, he was skilled enough to join the sports troop of the People's Liberation Army and by the time he turned eighteen, he had made a place for himself on the Chinese national badminton team.

Dan's first international success came in 2000 when he won both the singles as well as the team events at the Asia Junior Championships. However, it would be another four years before the world would get to see the true flowering of Dan's genius.

In 2004, he reached the top of the BWF rankings and then went on to cement his position by winning the Swiss Open as well as the All England Open. The Olympic medal, though, eluded him as Dan was ousted early from the Athens Games.

He would have to wait till 2008 to realize his dreams of winning at the Olympic Games. That year at Beijing, he won his first Olympic gold medal and then repeated the feat at London in 2012—thus becoming the first and only badminton player to successfully defend the singles title in the history of the Games.

In the meantime, Dan was sweeping away all the other major titles of the badminton world. He won each of the world championships, the Sudirman Cup and the Thomas Cup a phenomenal five times, besides winning the gold medal at the Asia Championships and the Asian Games four times each. Like the Olympics, he has twice been the World Cup champion too.

Being under constant limelight, Dan is highly protective of his personal life. He had a secret engagement with fellow badminton player Xie Xingfang in December 2010 after which the couple were married in September 2012. In November 2016, Dan and his wife welcomed their first child—a baby girl—into the world.

Dan has been honoured with various awards because of his superlative performances on the badminton court. For two years straight—in 2006 and 2007—he was presented with the 'Eddie Choong Player of the Year' award while the 2010 Asian Games saw him voted the 'Most Valuable Player'. In 2011, Dan was voted the male recipient of the CCTV 'Sports Personality of the Year', in recognition of his dominance at the major badminton titles of 2010.

- Dan was initially encouraged by his parents to learn piano.
- In 2012, he accepted his master's degree at Huaqiao University, thus becoming China's first active badminton player with a master's degree.

LIONEL MESSI

Argentina-born Lionel Messi is widely regarded as the most successful footballer of these times. In 2012, he scored a total of 91 goals—thereby, setting the record for the maximum number of goals in a calendar year. Messi has won the FIFA 'World Player of the Year' award in 2009 and the joint FIFA/Ballon d'Or (Golden Ball) award five times.

Born on 24 June 1987, in Rosario, Argentina, as Luis Lionel Andres Messi, the future football star was naturally gifted with speed, skill and agility right from early childhood.

As a fourteen-year-old, Messi thus began playing in the FC Barcelona junior team but such was his prowess with the ball, that only two years later, he made his debut in the regular team. At seventeen years of age, he set a record for being the youngest footballer as well as goal scorer in the Spanish La Liga. Despite being granted Spanish citizenship in 2005, he continued to maintain strong ties with his country of origin and the same year, he helped Argentina win the under-20 World Cup.

Messi led the Argentine national team to an Olympic gold medal in Beijing in 2008. In the final of the 2014 World Cup, Messi managed to steer Argentina to the finals but they eventually lost to Germany, though he was later honoured with the Golden Ball award—the award for the best player of the tournament.

Messi earned some of his best goals for his club, FC Barcelona. 2009 proved to be a particularly successful year as Barcelona won

La Liga, the Champions League, as well as the Spanish Super Cup titles. Again in 2010 and 2011, he would lead his club to La Liga and the Spanish Super Cup championships. In 2011, he would help Barcelona to win the Champions League title. In 2015, Messi led Barcelona to victory again in the holy trinity of European football—La Liga, Champions League and the Spanish Super Cup.

However, his run on the Argentine team was not so successful and after a series of losses suffered by the team in the 2015–16 season, Messi announced his retirement from international football. The departure lasted only for a few months though and soon he returned to the national squad, helping it to qualify for the 2018 World Cup with a stunning hat-trick against Ecuador in October 2017—the forty-fourth of his career. The achievement was especially welcome in the wake of a series of professional and personal setbacks in 2016, as in July that year, he and his father were indicted by a Barcelona court for tax fraud.

Despite ups and downs, Messi continues his dominance in the world of football. Having won the FIFA/Ballon d'Or for a record five times and setting several other records for the number of goals scored, he is famous for his agile footwork, creative play and nimble passes. The left-footed footballer is also a child rights activist and in 2007, he founded the Leo Messi Foundation with the goal of opening up opportunities to disadvantaged youths. He has also been named the United Nations International Children's Emergency Fund (UNICEF) goodwill ambassador for his active support of children's rights worldwide.

- When Messi failed to attain growth like other kids of his age, his parents took him to a doctor whereupon he was diagnosed with a type of hormone deficiency. Treatment in Argentina proved expensive for his middle-class parents but impressed by young Messi's potential, the FC Barcelona club offered to bear the costs.

- Messi celebrates his goals by looking up and pointing to the sky in tribute to his grandmother, who had left a lasting impression on him, and had died shortly before his eleventh birthday.

MAGIC JOHNSON

American basketball player Magic Johnson dominated the sport during the 1980s. He led his club Los Angeles Lakers to as many as five NBA championship titles over a twelve-year-long career.

Born as Earvin Johnson Jr., on 14 August 1959, in Lansing, Michigan, the future basketball champion grew up amongst nine brothers and sisters.

After helping his high school team win a state championship title in 1977, Johnson enrolled in Michigan State University which too, benefited from his excellent ball-handling skills and went on to win the 1979 NCAA championship. These college years also saw the beginning of Johnson's on-court rivalry with another basketball legend, Larry Bird, who later joined Boston Celtics. The matches between the Los Angeles Lakers and Boston Celtics in the 1980s unleashed a new wave of popularity for the NBA.

In his sophomore year however, Johnson left college and joined Los Angeles Lakers who picked him in the first overall 1979 NBA draft. This was the beginning of a twelve-year-long association during which Los Angeles Lakers won the NBA championship title as many as five times. In fact, the first came in Johnson's rookie season with which he set a record of being the first rookie to win the NBA finals' 'Most Valuable Player' award—an honour that he would go on to win two more times. Apart from this, Johnson would be decorated with the League 'Most Valuable Player' title three times—in 1987, 1989 and 1990.

Towering at six-feet nine-inches, Johnson was not only well-placed to score from anywhere on the court but was adept in rebounds as well. However, what drove the crowds wild were his creative passes as well as his instinct for big scores under pressure.

In November 1991, Johnson stunned the sports world by announcing that he was HIV positive and was exiting professional basketball. However, he was part of the 1992 American Dream Team that won the gold medal at the Barcelona Olympics and for a very brief while in 1996, came back to Los Angeles Lakers. After fully retiring from the sport the same year, he established himself as a successful businessman and also started the Magic Johnson Foundation to promote research and awareness efforts in the field of HIV and AIDS.

- While attending Everett High School, the young Johnson once scored 36 points, 16 rebounds as well as 16 assists in a single game–a feat that led to a sports reporter to describe him as 'Magic'. The epithet stuck and young Earvin began to be known as Magic Johnson.

- In 1992, Johnson wrote the a guide book called *What You Can Do To Avoid AIDS*.

MA LONG

Chinese table tennis player Ma Long is the present Olympic as well as World Champion in the sport. Till August 2017, he was also at the top of the International Table Tennis Federation (ITTF) rankings—a spot he had retained for thirty consecutive months (from March 2015), besides holding it overall for sixty months. After winning the men's singles at the 2016 Olympics, Ma Long also became the only male player to have won every singles title in table tennis.

Born on 20 October 1988 in Anshan, the Liaoning province of China, Ma Long picked up table tennis when he was only five years old. After eight years, he arrived in Beijing to begin a more advanced level of training and by 2003, he was competent enough to be selected for the Chinese national team. The very next year, Long won the World Junior Championships and all the three events at the 2004 Asian Junior Championships held in New Delhi.

In 2006, Long bagged the World Team Championships title and with it, he also set the record for being the youngest player to win the title. Since then he has gone on to win another nine gold medals at the World Championships, six of which have been in the team event, one in doubles and two in singles.

Long's Olympic journey, however, had not been so smooth. Despite playing well for most of 2011 and 2012, he was not allowed to participate in the singles event at the 2012 London

Olympics due to a brief dip in performance and had to be satisfied with a gold medal for the team event. However, in 2016, in Rio de Janeiro, Long proved his world dominance in the sport by winning two gold medals at the Olympic Games in the singles as well as the team events.

Long has won eight World Cup titles in his career—of which six have come from the team event and two in singles. In the Asian Games, Long has garnered five gold medals—three in team events, two in doubles and one in singles.

For a time in his career—especially leading to the 2012 London Olympics—Long had to contend with doubts about his ability to deal with the intense psychological pressure of most crucial games. A streak of losses in finals of singles events at that time led experts to question his resilience. However, Long proved his detractors wrong and with his 2016 Olympic singles gold as well as the 2017 World Championship men's singles at Düsseldorf, he is now the undisputed champion of world table tennis.

- Long bears the nickname, 'Flying Dragon', reportedly because, as per Chinese astrology, he was born in the Year of the Dragon.

- He graduated from Shanghai Jiao Tong University with a degree in Economics and Management, completed over a span of six years, instead of the usual four, due to his busy schedule.

MARK SPITZ

Mark Spitz is a former American swimming champion who, in 1972, shot into limelight for being the first athlete to win seven gold medals in a single Olympic Games.

Born as Mark Andrew Spitz on 10 February 1950 in Modesto, California, the future swimming sensation took to water as early as a two-year-old when his family moved to Hawaii. After four years though, the family moved back to California where young Mark started swimming competitively. Around this time he also started training under the widely respected coach, Sherm Chavoor, at the Arden Hills Swim Club in Sacramento.

By 1960, Spitz had proved himself as the world's best swimmer in the under-10 category. As a mere ten-year-old, he already had a world record under his belt besides seventeen national records in his age categories. In the 1967 Pan-American Games held in Winnipeg, Canada, Spitz won a whopping five gold medals and showed the world that he was ready for the Olympic Games.

In Mexico City next year, Spitz did not disappoint and he won a total of four medals at the Olympics—two gold in team events, a silver in the 100 metre butterfly as well as a bronze in the 100 metre freestyle.

However, the lack of a gold medal in an individual capacity bothered Spitz. After returning home, he sought out superior training facilities even as he enrolled for a pre-dental degree at the Indiana University.

By the time the world's athletes converged in Munich for the 1972 Olympic Games, Spitz was better prepared. And he proved it with an incredible haul of seven gold medals in various swimming events. What's more, he even set new records in all the four events that he entered—these including the 100 metre freestyle and butterfly as well as the 200 metre freestyle and butterfly.

Spitz leveraged his Olympic success to get lucrative endorsement deals and by 1974, he was making as much as $6 million. He also attempted a career in Hollywood but gave it up after his initial attempts at acting failed. Eventually, he established a real estate business and became a motivational speaker.

In 1992, Spitz tried to return to competitive swimming by entering the 50 metre butterfly event, but failed to qualify for the Olympic team. However, his record of seven gold medals in a single Olympic Games remained unbroken for thirty-six years; only in 2008 did fellow American Michael Phelps win eight gold medals at the Beijing Olympics. Over his career, he was feted as the 'World Swimmer of the Year' three times—in 1969, 1971 and 1972—by the *Swimming World* magazine. In 1977, Spitz was inducted into the International Swimming Hall of Fame and in 1983, he found a place for himself in the United States Olympic Hall of Fame.

- Spitz's glory in the 1972 Olympics was temporarily overshadowed by the kidnapping and murder of seven Israeli Olympic athletes by Palestinian terrorists because of which he was hastily flown back to the United States, even before the official closing of the Olympic Games.

- A photograph of him wearing a swimsuit and with his seven gold medals was made into a poster, and it quickly became a bestseller.

MARTINA NAVRATILOVA

Women's tennis icon of the 1970s and '80s, Martina Navratilova won an incredible fifty-six Grand Slam championship titles during her career, including eighteen singles, of which a record nine came from the grass court Mecca—Wimbledon. Along with tennis statistics, Navratilova is remembered today as a pioneer of women's sports, who proved that female players can play with as much power and strength as their male counterparts.

Navratilova was born in Prague on 18 October 1956. Even though she was interested in a variety of sports such as soccer, hockey and skiing since childhood, it was tennis that she was most passionate about. When she was only fifteen, she won the Czech National Championship after which she turned professional. Though unseeded at the time, she appeared in the 1973 French Open and reached till the quarter-finals.

A couple of years later, Navratilova defected to the United States and in 1981, she got her American citizenship. In 1978, she won her first Grand Slam tournament after defeating Chris Evert in the Wimbledon finals. From 1982 to 1987, Navratilova would sweep the Wimbledon championships for six straight years. In fact, her last singles Grand Slam win would once more be at the Wimbledon where she would beat Zina Garrison in the 1990 women's singles finals.

Navratilova lifted the US Open Cup four times, the French Open, twice, and the Australian Open, three times. Unfortunately, the single season Grand Slam series would always elude her, though there would be no one to dispute her dominance in women's tennis during the early 1980s.

From the second half of the 1990s, Navratilova was more successful in the doubles category. In 2003, she won the mixed-doubles championship at Wimbledon and in 2006, at the US Open. Over the course of her career, Navratilova would go on to win thirty-one titles in ladies doubles championships and ten Grand Slam mixed-doubles titles in all.

After retiring from competitive tennis, Navratilova became involved with issues close to her heart, such as gay rights, underprivileged children as well as animal rights. Though some of her records remain unbeaten—such as most WTA singles titles (167) and most doubles titles (177) in the Open Era[*]—her real legacy was the way she revolutionized women's tennis. Shrugging off the tamer pace of her predecessors who rarely moved beyond the baseline, Navratilova used deadly serves and fierce volleys to bring passion and energy to the sport and showed that women could play with physical strength and power as well.

---

[*]The Open Era in tennis began from April 1968 when professional players were allowed to compete in the Grand Slam tournaments. Prior to this, the Grand Slam tournaments allowed only amateurs—in other words, players did not get any prize money.

- Martina's grandmother was a tennis player who had represented Czechoslovakia before the Second World War.
- She has written three mystery-thriller novels with author Liz Nickles: *The Total Zone, Breaking Point and Killer Instinct.*

M.C. MARY KOM

Mary Kom is an Indian sports icon who is a five-time winner of the World Amateur Boxing Championship as well as the only female boxer to have won a medal in each of the six world championships. Nicknamed 'Magnificent Mary', she did her country proud by not only being the sole woman to qualify for the 2012 Olympic Games but even returning from London with an Olympic bronze medal in the flyweight category.

Born on 1 March 1983, as Mangte Chungneijang of the Kom tribe in the north-eastern Indian state of Manipur, the future boxing champion adopted the name Mary Kom once she began to garner fame as a boxer. Life was busy for young Mary as she not only helped to bring up her four younger siblings at home but also worked on the fields alongside her parents.

Despite her parents' opposition—as boxing was considered too masculine and hence an unsuitable sport for a young girl—Mary Kom travelled to the Manipur State Boxing Institute in Imphal. There she met coach M. Narjit Singh and persuaded him to give her a chance at training. Mary's passion for the sport soon became evident to all as she would often train till late in the evening—after everyone else had left the institute.

Mary's hard work bore the first fruit in 2000 when she won the 'Best Boxer' award at the first State Boxing Championships. Soon enough she stormed to the national levels and from 2000 to 2005, she won a total of five National Championship titles. Her first major international competition was the 45 kg category at the 2001 International Boxing Association (AIBA) Women's World Boxing Championship where she came 2nd. However, in 2002, she would win the gold medal in the event and would repeat the feat successively four more times—in 2005, 2006, 2008 and 2010—though in the last, she would compete in the 48 kg category.

Mary Kom's AIBA Women's World Boxing Championship titles were even more praiseworthy as the last two came after she became a mother to two children. Furthermore, the 2010 win paved the way for the 2012 Olympic Games which was historic since it would be the first time women's boxing would be allowed in the Olympics. In London, Mary Kom won a bronze medal in the flyweight though she had to shift to the 51 kg bracket which was the lowest of the three weight categories allowed in the Olympics.

Apart from the world stage, Mary Kom has won the Asian Women's Boxing Championship four times. In the 2009 Asian Indoor Games at Hanoi, she won the gold medal in the pinweight category and in the 2014 Asian Games at Incheon, she again won the gold medal in the flyweight event.

In recognition for her immense contribution to women's boxing in India, Mary Kom has been feted with the Arjuna Award in 2003, Padma Shri in 2006 and the Padma Bhushan in 2013—all among the highest State honours awarded to civilians by the Government of India. In this way, a girl from a small village not only made it big in the predominantly male world of boxing but through her never-say-die spirit, became an inspiration for hundreds of girls in India to take up the sport.

- At school, Mary Kom displayed avid interest in sports and would eagerly participate in football, hockey and athletics–in fact, she never tried out boxing at school. She got hooked to the sport only after fellow Manipuri and boxer, Dingko Singh, won a gold medal at the 1998 Asian Games.

- Mary Kom's family found out about her boxing skills after a local newspaper wrote about her state championship title.

- Her trailblazing achievements found further popularity with the release of her biopic titled *Mary Kom* and starring former beauty-queen-turned-international-actress, Priyanka Chopra.

MICHAEL JOHNSON

American sprinter Michael Johnson was the most successful name in track and field events of the 1990s. In 1996, he became the first athlete to win gold medals in two different distances in a single Olympic Games, besides setting new Olympic records in both events. By the time he retired in 2008, Johnson had under his belt, five Olympic gold medals as well as nine IAAF world championship titles.

Michael Johnson was born on 13 September 1967, in Dallas, Texas. Like his four other siblings, young Michael was into sports, but unlike them, he developed a keener interest in running rather than contact sports such as basketball and football. Though he was on the track team at his school, Johnson never took the sport as a career option and actually wanted to become an architect.

It was not until he enrolled in Baylor University, that Johnson was spotted by coach Clyde Hart as much as for his potential as a runner as for his mature approach to life. By the time he graduated in 1990 with a bachelor's degree in accounting and marketing, Johnson had made a name for himself as the fastest man in both the 200 metre and 400 metre sprints.

Johnson's first major international victory came in the 1991 World Championships where he won both the indoor and outdoor 200 metre sprint and set a new world record in the former event. The Olympic Games held next year at Barcelona however, proved something of a disappointment as Johnson could not win an individual gold though he was part of the gold-medal-winning 4×400 metre relay team that had set a new world record too.

Once again in the 1995 World Championships, Johnson not only won both long sprints but twice set new world records in the indoor 400 metres event. The 1996 Atlanta Olympic Games turned out to be the peak of his running career since he not only won gold medals in 200 metre and 400 metre sprints but also set a new world mark in the former with his time of 19.32 seconds.

Four years later, Johnson became the first male Olympic sprinter to defend his 400 metre gold medal in Sydney apart from winning another gold medal as the anchor of the 4×400 metre relay team.

Johnson retired from competitive running in 2001 right after winning a gold medal in the 4×400 relay event at the Goodwill Games held that year in Brisbane, Australia. Many sports experts, including his long-time coach Clyde Hart, believed that Johnson had bid farewell to the track at the right time. In 2004, he was inducted into the United States Track and Field Hall of Fame, where his 1996 Olympic win in the 200 metre sprint was lauded as the greatest track and field moment of the last twenty-five years.

- In 2008, with the revelation that one of his relay teammates had taken illegal performance-enhancing drugs, Johnson returned the relay gold medal–though technically he was not under any obligation to do so.

- Michael Johnson's unique running stance–a stiff back and short steps–has often been likened by sports reporters to that of a 'running duck.'

MICHAEL JORDAN

American basketball legend Michael Jordan is recognized all over the world as the sport's most successful and NBA's most decorated player. He is a five-time winner of high profile leagues' 'Most Valuable Player' and a three-time winner of their 'All Star Most Valuable Player'.

Michael Jordan was born on 17 February 1963, in Brooklyn, New York, though the family soon moved to Wilmington, North Carolina. At the Emsley A. Laney High School, young Jordan played a variety of sports such as baseball and football, though it was clear that his passion lay in basketball. Not surprisingly then, after he joined University of North Carolina at Chapel Hill, Jordan became the driving force of his college basketball team, guiding it to several victories, such as the 1982 NCAA Division I championship, besides being declared the NCAA 'College Player of the Year' for two straight years—1983 and 1984.

1984 was also the year of the Los Angeles Olympics and Jordan's scoring skills went a long way in helping the home team win the gold medal. Eight years later, Jordan once again played a star role in the United States basketball team as it returned from Barcelona with the Olympic gold medal.

In the meantime, Jordan's NBA career was touching lofty heights. After being inducted into the Chicago Bulls in 1984, he ended the season by bagging NBA's 'Rookie of the Year' award as well as an entry into the All-Star Game. However, it was in the season of 1986–87 that Jordan really came into his own. An unstoppable force on the court, Jordan scored a 3,041 whopping points over the season, thus becoming the first player since Wilt Chamberlin in 1963 to cross the 3,000 mark in a single season. Expectedly, he was named NBA's 'Most Valuable Player' title that year—an honour which he would win another four times in his league career—for two successive years in 1991 and 1992 and later again in 1996 and 1998.

Fired by Jordan's brilliance on court, Chicago Bulls went on to dominate the pro basketball circuit in the early 1990s. For three consecutive years—1991, 1992 and 1993—Jordan helped the Bulls to win the NBA championships. But then tragedy struck Jordan's family—in July 1993 he lost his father to street robbery. Shattered by this loss, Jordan announced a sabbatical from pro basketball and instead joined Birmingham Barons, a minor baseball league team, as an outfielder.

In 1995, Jordan returned to Chicago Bulls and helped his team win the NBA championships in the 1995–96 season. He was now at the pinnacle of his league career and the Bulls benefited by winning the NBA championship titles for another two successive years—1997 and 1998. This was followed by a brief hiatus, after which Jordan signed up with Washington Wildcats. In 2003, however he permanently retired from professional basketball though he continues to be associated with the sport in his capacity as part-owner of Charlotte Bobcats.

Nicknamed 'Air Jordan' and 'His Airness', Michael Jordan mesmerized basketball fans with his incredible leaps and ability to score baskets. Many current NBA stars such as LeBron James and Dwayne Wade admit that Jordan's genius has had a decisive influence on their careers. He had famously once said, 'One day, you might look up and see me playing the game at fifty.

Don't laugh. Never say never, because limits, like fears, are often just an illusion,' and just this one quote portrays why Michael Jordan is such a legend.

- Such was Jordan's passion for the sport, that he was the only NBA player to have included a special 'Love of the Game' clause into his contract, which meant that he could never be prevented from playing basketball against anyone, at anytime and anywhere.
- Swimming is one of Michael Jordan's biggest fears.

MICHAEL PHELPS

American swimmer Michael Phelps may be described as the fastest man in water. Though he holds several world records in swimming, two of the most high-profile ones are for the most number of medals won in the history of Olympic Games as well for winning maximum number of individual gold medals during a single Olympic Games.

Born on 30 June 1985, in Baltimore, United States, young Phelps first ventured to the pool while tagging along after his older sisters, Whitney and Hilary, to the local swimming team.

The first major stepping stone on Phelps's path to success was his selection in 1999 to the US National B team which was soon followed by his appearance at Sydney for the 2000 Olympics at the age of just fifteen. Though he did not win any medal in the Olympics, at the 2001 World Championships, he set a record in the 200 metre butterfly, thus becoming—at fifteen years and nine months—the youngest to achieve such a feat.

This was only the beginning of a record-breaking spree that saw Phelps sweep successive World Championships in 2002 and 2003. 2004 marked the rise of a phenomenal swimmer on the Olympic stage as he returned from Athens with eight medals, including six gold. In 2007, he reaffirmed his superstar status in the world of swimming by winning gold medals at the World Aquatic Championships in Melbourne, Australia, and breaking five world records in the process.

The year 2008 turned out to be the best year for Phelps professionally as he swept the Beijing Olympics by winning the gold medal in as many as eight different events. Along the way, he set new world records in all events apart from the 100 metre butterfly in which he set a new Olympic record. Four years later at London, he added another four gold medals to his Olympic tally. Soon after the Games, he was honoured as the most decorated Olympic athlete by FINA. Four years later, Phelps won five gold medals at the Rio Olympics after which he signalled his retirement from competitive swimming.

Phelps however, has faced several challenges in his personal life, especially struggling with alcohol abuse which even led to his suspension from the 2015 World Aquatic Championships. But like a true sportsperson, he has repeatedly emerged from his crises by dint of hard work, dedicated training and passion for swimming. Today, with a tally of twenty-eight Olympic medals—including twenty-three gold medals—he is the most decorated athlete in the history of the Games and an inspiration for generations of sportspersons to come.

- Seven-year-old Michael was initially a little nervous about being completely under water. However, things became much more enjoyable after he began to float on his back–as suggested by his instructor–and soon enough, young Phelps became an expert in the backstroke and was well on his way to making history.

- With a capacity of 12 litres, Phelps's lungs are nearly twice the size of an average human's.

MICHAEL SCHUMACHER

Former German auto racing star Michael Schumacher is widely regarded as one of the greatest F1 drivers of all time. Apart from winning the F1 championship an incredible seven times, he has also set world records for most wins and most championship points in F1 racing. In 2013, Schumacher suffered a serious head injury in a skiing accident and currently he is on the path to rehabilitation.

Born on 3 January 1969 in Hurth, Germany, Schumacher gave evidence of his passion for racing as early as a four-year-old, whereupon his father modified his pedal kart by adding a small motorcycle engine.

In 1984 and 1985, Schumacher won the German Junior Kart Championship. Four years later, he made his single-seat car racing debut in the German Formula Ford and even went on to win the Formula Konig that year. By 1989, he was confident enough in the F3 arena and joined Willi Weber's Weber-Trella Stuttgart (WTS) F3 team and the very next year, won the German F3 title too. However instead of rushing to enter F1 racing, Schumacher decided to prepare himself to drive powerful cars over long-distance races by signing up with the Mercedes junior racing programme in the World Sports-Prototype Championship.

Schumacher's plan paid off and soon after making his F1 debut at the 1991 Belgian Grand Prix, he won the World Drivers' Championship for the Benetton–Ford team both in 1994 and

1995. In 1996, he joined Ferrari and with them, began a long productive association that would see Schumacher touch the heights of F1 glory. From 2000 to 2004, every year Schumacher won the F1 championship. At the end of the 2006 season, with a staggering ninety-one F1 Grand Prix race victories under his belt that left previous record-holder Alain Prost's fifty-one far behind, Schumacher announced his retirement from active racing.

However, in December 2009, Schumacher decided to come back to F1 racing with the Mercedes team, though the association would not be much successful. He decided to retire for good in 2012 and soon got busy, first with research such as developing the first lightweight carbon helmet by teaming up with Schuberth and later, with his philanthropic initiatives.

In December 2013, while skiing in France, Schumacher suffered a serious head injury and had to be placed in a medically-induced coma till June 2014. In September the same year, he was brought back home to continue the rehabilitation process.

Schumacher has been feted throughout the world for his racing prowess. He is a two-time winner of the Laureus 'World Sportsman of the Year' award and in 2006 he was awarded a Fédération Internationale de l'Automobile (FIA) Gold Medal for Motor Sport. In 2010, he was honoured with the 'Chevalier of the French Legion of Honour' by then French prime minister, François Fillon, and the Millennium Trophy was conferred on him at the Bambi Awards on 13 November 2013, less than a month before from his near-fatal accident.

- So eager was young Schumacher to get his kart licence, that he decided to go to Luxembourg from where he could obtain it at twelve years old, rather than waiting to turn fourteen, which was the minimum age at which he could get it in Germany.

- Schumacher considered an African beaded bracelet gifted to him by his wife as his lucky charm and carried it to every race. After the skiing accident, the charm was found buried in snow at the site of the accident.

MIKE TYSON

American professional boxer Mike Tyson dominated the heavyweight boxing rings from 1985 to 2005. He first shot to fame when he won the heavyweight championship title in 1986. Thus, at mere twenty years of age, he became the youngest boxer to do so.

Born as Michael Jordan Tyson on 30 June 1966, in Brooklyn, New York, the future boxing champion did not have an easy childhood. When he was only two, his father abandoned the family and it was left to his mother to bring up three children singlehandedly. By the time young Mike, as he was called, was eleven, he had already become part of street gangs and engaged in criminal activity. After being arrested several times, young Tyson was sent to a reform school known as Tyron School for Boys where his boxing potential was spotted by social worker and boxing enthusiast Bobby Stewart. He agreed to teach Tyson everything that he knew about boxing on the condition that the young man worked hard at his studies and gave up criminal activities. Tyson began to improve on all counts and Stewart then introduced the budding boxer to famous boxing manager, Constantine D'Amato.

In 1984, Tyson failed to qualify for the Olympic Games trials after which Amato decided that the young boxer should turn professional. The gamble paid off and on 22 November 1986, Tyson defeated Trevor Berbick in a second-round knockout. Not only did he win the World Boxing Council championship but also emerged as the youngest heavyweight champion in history.

Clearly, Mike Tyson was now on the path to fame. In March 1987, he defeated James Smith to win the World Boxing Association (WBA) belt and in August the same year, he pummelled Tony Tucker to claim the International Boxing Federation title as well. With this, Tyson—now nicknamed 'Iron Mike'—was the undisputed king of world heavyweight boxing. Even more incredibly, Tyson would go on to defend his heavyweight title successfully as many as ten times.

However, Tyson would be unable to handle the sudden shower of fame and wealth and would soon start losing control of both his personal and professional life at the same time. His marriage to small-time actress Robin Givens would become embroiled in a series of domestic abuse charges and he would also find himself at odds with his trainers and managers. Things came to a head in 1992 when Tyson was convicted on charges of raping a beauty pageant contestant.

After his release from prison in 1995, Tyson tried to reclaim his position as the heavyweight champion and even won two of his titles back but lost his boxing licence due to his shocking behaviour in a match against Evander Holyfield. On 28 June 1997, the two met at the MGM Grand Garden Arena of Las Vegas to claim the WBA Heavyweight Championship. In one of the most bizarre events in world sports, Tyson first bit off a piece of cartilage from Holyfield's right ear and then again, after a time-out, bit Holyfield's left ear. After the time expired, the second bite was discovered and Tyson was disqualified from the match.

Tyson's professional and personal troubles continued and in 2003 he had his last professional win. However in 2013, Tyson revealed to the world that he has been fighting substance abuse and with that, held out hope that he would be able to put difficult times behind him and re-invent himself in a more positive role.

- Constantine D'Amato was not only Tyson's boxing coach but was also his legal guardian.
- Tyson performed a solo stage show called 'Mike Tyson: Undisputed Truth', which he first presented in Las Vegas in 2012.

MILKHA SINGH

Known as the 'Flying Sikh', Milkha Singh brought India its first athletics gold medal in the history of Commonwealth Games besides being the country's first sprinter to run at the finals of an Olympic event.

After a difficult childhood spent living with relatives and in migrant camps, young Milkha joined the army. It was in the services that he discovered his talent for running and won the national trials in the 200 metre and 400 metre sprint for the 1956 Melbourne Olympics.

At Melbourne though, Singh, because of his relative inexperience and lack of professional training, could not progress beyond the heats. However, two years later, at the 1958 Asian Games, Singh won both the 200 metre and 400 metre sprint. Even more significantly, the same year, he came first in the 440 yard race at the Commonwealth Games. Thus, he became the first Commonwealth Games gold medallist from independent India as well as the only individual Indian athlete to do so till as late as 2014.

In Rome for the 1960 Olympics, Singh missed the 3rd place in the 400 metre sprint by a whisker but still turned out to be the first Indian to have participated in the finals of an Olympic track and field event. He again tried for the 1964 Tokyo Olympics but was unable to clear the preliminary heats.

The Asian Games however, proved more successful for Singh

as he won the 400 metre sprint again in 1962 besides being part of the gold-medal winning Indian relay team at Jakarta.

After retiring from competitive running, Singh continued to be associated with athletics in an administrative capacity and became the Director of Sports in the Punjab Ministry of Education—a post he held till his retirement in 1998. In an effort to discover sporting talents among children from disadvantaged backgrounds, he also founded the Milkha Singh Charitable Trust in 2003. For his contribution to Indian athletics, Milkha Singh has been honoured with numerous awards, including the Padma Shri in 1959 by the President of India.

- The exact year of Milkha Singh's birth is uncertain—some records show 1929 while others put it as 1935—since he was orphaned during the India-Pakistan Partition of 1947.

- For the biopic based on him, Milkha Singh charged only ₹1 from the producers.

- Then Pakistan President, General Ayub Khan, praised his win in 1960, saying, 'Milkha, you did not run; you flew'. Ever since, the Indian athlete has been known as the 'Flying Sikh'.

MUHAMMAD ALI

Former American boxer Muhammad Ali is now recognized as a legendary figure in the sport, whose success—such as the 1960 Olympic gold medal and the 1964 world heavyweight boxing championship—not only brought him personal fame but also inspired other African Americans to struggle to emerge from the shadow of racial discrimination.

Born as Cassius Marcellus Clay Jr. on 17 January 1942, in Louisville, Kentucky, Ali grew up at a time when life was hard for people of African origin. With so little to be happy about in his life, when young Clay found his bicycle stolen, he raged to Louisville police officer Joe Martin. He apparently added that he would like to beat up the thief. 'Well, you better learn how to fight before you start challenging people,' Martin reportedly responded. Clay took the advice to heart and began training as a boxer under Martin himself.

Soon Clay won two national Golden Gloves titles for novices in the light heavyweight class, the National Golden Gloves Tournament of Champions title and then the AAU's national title for the light heavyweight division—all at eighteen. The peak of his amateur career came in 1960 when at Rome, he defeated Polish boxer Zbigniew Pietrzykowski to claim the Olympic gold medal in the light heavyweight category.

Upon his return to the US, Clay decided to go pro and by 1963, had delivered as many as fifteen knockouts in his first nineteen fights. In 1964, he defeated Sonny Liston to become the new heavyweight champion of the world. The professional elevation was accompanied by a new personal avatar too, as Clay joined the Nation of Islam and took on the name of Muhammad Ali. This decision further impacted his professional choices as he refused to serve in the United States Army during the Vietnam War, saying, 'My conscience won't let me go shoot my brother, or some darker people, or some poor hungry people in the mud for big powerful America'. Consequently, he was arrested and had his boxing licence suspended by the New York State Athletic Commission. After a long legal fight, Ali was able to return to professional boxing after the United States Supreme Court overturned the conviction in June 1971. Of Ali's victory, former United States Attorney General Eric Holder, later said, 'His biggest win came not in the ring but in our courts in his fight for his beliefs.'

The same year—on 8 March—Ali met reigning heavyweight champ Joe Frazier in what came to be known as the 'Fight of the Century'. Though Ali lost this match but three years later, on 30 October 1974, at a fight in Kinshasa, Zaire, billed as the 'Rumble in the Jungle', Ali, now thirty-two, managed to defeat twenty-five-year-old George Foreman and reclaim the World Heavyweight Champion title. Frazier and Ali met again next year in a long gruelling match nicknamed 'Thrilla in Manila,' in Quezon City, Philippines, which ended with Ali winning. In September 1978, Ali became the first boxer to win the heavyweight championship three times, when he overcame Leon Spinks in a unanimous fifteen-round decision to win back the heavyweight title.

However, a series of losses soon convinced an ageing Ali to bid goodbye to the boxing ring in December 1981. Despite being diagnosed with Parkinson's disease and increasingly restricted by his physical condition, Ali continued to head several philanthropic initiatives till he passed away in June 2016. In 1999, he was voted the BBC 'Sporting Personality of the Century', and in 2005 he was honoured with the Presidential Medal of Freedom from then President George W. Bush. Apart from his boxing success—underlined by an enviable career tally of fifty-six wins, five losses and thirty-seven knockouts—his real legacy was to inspire an entire generation of Americans to overthrow the shackles of racial discrimination and to practise in life, the truest values of sportsmanship and fair play.

- Before his 1964 fight with Liston, a precocious Ali said that he intended to 'float like a butterfly, sting like a bee'–words which eventually went on to immortalize his boxing style.

- Ali's refusal to being drafted in the Vietnam War was one of the sources of inspiration for great civil rights activist, Martin Luther King Jr.'s later opposition to the War.

NADIA COMANECI

Nadia Comaneci is best remembered today for being the first gymnast to be awarded a score of 10 in the history of Olympics. The feat, achieved at the 1976 Montreal Olympics, when she was just fourteen years old, shot Comaneci into the limelight after which she went on to win five Olympic gold medals in her career.

Born on 12 November 1961, in Onesti, Romania, Nadia Elena Comaneci was fascinated by gymnastics right from her kindergarten days and was part of a local team called Flacara. Her innate talent was spotted by then famous Romanian gymnast Béla Károlyi, who would later go on to coach the national team. In 1968, young Nadia joined Károlyi's gymnastics school and just two years later, she won the 1970 Romanian Nationals. At just nine years of age, she became the youngest gymnast to do so.

Comaneci made her international debut in 1971 by entering a dual junior meet between Romania and Yugoslavia. Here, she not only attained her first all-around title but helped her team win the gold medal as well. After many junior titles, Comaneci entered her first major tournament in 1975 at the European Championships that was being hosted in Skien, Norway. She swept off the meet, winning gold medals in every event (apart from the floor exercise in which she bagged silver), and winning the all-round crown as well.

Riding high on the success of several pre-Olympic tournaments such as the American Cup and the Chunichi Cup, Comaneci was a favourite at the 1976 Olympics. And sure enough, she mesmerized Montreal with a perfect 10 performance as many as seven times besides winning three gold medals, one silver and one bronze. Predictably enough, the world went into a tizzy covering the sensational success of a fourteen-year-old girl from behind the Iron Curtain. Though initially Comaneci received many public honours in her own country too, increasing state interference coupled with personal issues brought about a sharp slide in her form at the 1978 World Championships. She bounced back with the 1979 European Championships, becoming the first gymnast, male or female, to win the title for the third successive time. Later, despite an infection on her hand, she helped Romania win a team gold medal at the 1979 World Championships too. The uneven performance trajectory was evident at the 1980 Olympic Games, where Comaneci won two gold and two silver medals. In 1981, she announced her retirement from competitive gymnastics and later took up coaching duties as part of the Romanian Gymnastics Federation.

In 1989, Comaneci made the bold decision to defect to the United States. Though it took her some time to get her bearings in the new country, she eventually found success as a model, businesswoman and after the fall of the Communist regime in Romania, as a philanthropist as well. Comaneci's legendary gymnastic skills are immortalized in the image of the fourteen-year-old girl delivering a perfect 10 performance at the balance beam in the 1976 Olympic Games.

- Comaneci was decorated with the Olympic Order in 1984 and 2004–thus, not only becoming its youngest recipient but also the only one to have received the highest Olympic honour twice.

- In her first Romanian National Championships, eight-year-old Nadia came 13th, upon which, her coach Béla Károlyi gave her a doll, saying it was unlucky to come 13th and she should never do that again.

NATALIE COUGHLIN

American swimmer Natalie Coughlin is one of the most famous names in the sport from modern times. She has won twelve Olympic medals and has broken many international swimming records.

Born on 23 August 1982, in Vallejo, California, to a police officer dad and a paralegal mom, Natalie took to water, when she was just ten months old, at their local YMCA pool. By the time she was six, Natalie was already swimming competitively and in high school, she was on her way towards setting new records. For example, the 1998 Summer National saw young Natalie qualifying for all its fourteen events—which made her the first high school swimmer to achieve such a feat.

In 2000, Coughlin graduated from high school and enrolled at the University of California, Berkeley, where her swimming prowess was fully honed by well-known coach Teri McKeever. Though a shoulder injury prevented her from trying for the 2000 Olympic Games, over the next three years, Coughlin swept away the NCAA swimming events—garnering not only twelve NCAA titles but also being named the NCAA 'Swimmer of the Year' for three straight years. That Coughlin was the new swimming sensation was amply clear when in 2002, she set the United States record at the 50 metre backstroke and went on to garner five national titles the same year.

By 2004, Coughlin was ready for the Olympic Games.

She returned from Athens with five medals, including breaking the Olympic 100 metre backstroke record twice. Coughlin continued her academic achievements as well and the following year, she graduated with a degree in psychology.

At Beijing, in 2008, Coughlin set another record for successfully defending her 100 metre backstroke gold in two straight Olympic Games.

In the 2011 World Championships held at Shanghai, Coughlin won a gold medal in the 100 metre medley relay, a silver in the 400 metre freestyle relay as well as a bronze in the 100 metre backstroke. The following year in London, Coughlin had to settle for an Olympic bronze medal in the 4×100 metre freestyle relay. By now, she was nearing thirty—a veteran age for competitive swimmers—and was being compelled to race against a much younger generation of swimmers.

Outside the pool however, Coughlin was still being showered with success and fame. She became quite a popular face on several TV shows, appearing as sports commentator, cookery show judge, talk-show host and in one of the most memorable appearances, as a competitor in the celebrity reality dance show, *Dancing with the Stars*.

Though Coughlin is no longer seen in major swimming competitions, her career achievements today inspire hundreds of budding swimmers around the world. Over her career, Coughlin racked up a total of sixty medals, besides being honoured with the 'World Swimmer of the Year' in 2002 and 'American Swimmer of the Year' three times—in 2001, 2002 and 2008.

- At the 2008 US Olympic Trials, Coughlin set a world record by finishing the 100 metre backstroke in 58.97 seconds—with this she became the only female swimmer in the world to have done it in less than a minute.

- Coughlin is fond of cooking, has appeared in Food Network's *Chopped* and judged *Iron Chef America*.

PAAVO NURMI

Finnish athlete Paavo Nurmi is remembered today as one of the greatest long-distance runners in the history of twentieth-century sports. He has a haul of nine gold medals and three silver ones in the Olympic Games of 1920, 1924 and 1928. This meant that he was the undisputed king of long-distance running in the 1920s, during which time, he also set a stupendous twenty-five world records in various distances.

Born as Paavo Johannes Nurmi on 13 June 1897, in the south-western Finnish port town of Turku, the future runner grew up in humble circumstances. During childhood, his natural athletic ability was honed by long runs through deep coniferous forests. When he was only thirteen, young Nurmi lost his father and was compelled to pick up jobs in the docks but still he excelled at school.

In the meantime, fellow Finn, Hannes Kolehmainen, brought glory to his country by winning three gold medals in long distance running at the 1912 Stockholm Olympics. Like hundreds of young men at the time, Nurmi—then only fifteen—was also inspired by Kolehmainen's achievements and decided to become an athlete.

Nurmi went about his dreams with the same systematic approach and unflagging perseverance that would later come to mark his running style. He joined a Turku sports club called Turun Urheiluliitto in 1914 and the same year, he set a national record by finishing the 3,000 metre race in 8 minutes and

36.2 seconds. With this, Finland realized that it had another running legend in the making.

Right enough, in the 1920 Olympic Games at Antwerp, Nurmi won the 10,000 metre run and the 10,000 metre cross-country race, besides the silver medal in 5,000 metre race. In 1923, he stunned the world by finishing the mile run in an incredible time of 4 minutes and 10.4 seconds—an international record that would hold good for the next eight years.

Nurmi reached the peak of his career in 1924 at the Paris Olympic Games. He not only successfully defended his 1920 Olympics 10,000 metre cross-country title but in fact, completed the 1,500 metre and 5,000 metre races within hours of each other and that too, in record timings that set new marks in the history of the Games. On the third consecutive day of his running, Nurmi once again helped Finland to win an unofficial 3,000 metre team race for which no medals were given. Nurmi returned to Finland to a hero's welcome and the next year, he embarked on a tour of the United States where he competed in a series of track and field meets. Nurmi's last appearance in an Olympic Games was in 1928; he returned from Amsterdam with a gold medal for his 10,000 metre win and two silver medals for his performances in the 5,000 metre and the 3,000 metre races. After the Olympics, he started running even longer distances and set new world records in the one hour run as well as the 25 mile marathon, even winning a gold medal for the latter like his idol Hannes Kolehmainen.

Paavo Nurmi is remembered today not only because of his twelve Olympic medals and twenty-five world records but also for his calm and mature technique. Running with a stopwatch, he would time himself evenly without bothering what other runners were doing. Eventually, this combination of genius and self-discipline made Nurmi a legend in the sport of long-distance running.

- Nurmi is the first and only runner to simultaneously hold world records in the mile, the 5,000 metre and the 10,000 metre races.

- He has various nicknames, such as 'The Flying Finn' and 'The King of Runners'.

PELE

Football legend Pele is regarded by many as perhaps the most creative exponent of the sport. More significantly, even after years of his retirement, Pele remains the only footballer to have been part of three World Cup winning teams.

Born as Edson Arantes do Nascimento on 23 October 1940, in Minas Gerais, Brazil, Pele grew up in a family with limited means.

When he was only eleven, Pele caught the attention of former Brazilian national-level player Waldemar de Brito, who took on the responsibility of training the boy. Soon Pele was selected by a local junior club, Baquinho, and next year, he joined one of the country's top clubs, Santos. After a spate of goals scored in league games as well as against Portuguese teams, in 1957, Pele was chosen to play on the Brazilian national team.

The very next year, Pele found himself heading to Sweden for the 1958 World Cup, making history by becoming the youngest player and goal-scorer ever in the tournament. His two goals in the finals helped Brazil to demolish Swedish defences and lift the World Cup. Despite an injury causing Pele to be out of action for most of the 1962 World Cup, Brazil won the finals against the Czech team. The injuries became more grievous in the 1966 World Cup as Pele repeatedly ended up as the target of on-field aggression. Brazil would have to wait till 1970 to win its third World Cup title. In the final against Italy, Pele scored the opening goal and made valuable assists which helped a star-studded Brazilian team to win the Cup in a most decisive manner.

In 1971, Pele stunned the world by announcing his retirement but soon became busy with various philanthropic initiatives and running a successful coffee business. Today, his fame not only rests on many personal records—such as scoring the highest number of career goals (1,283 goals from 1,363 first-class matches)—but also transforming football from being played in a primarily defensive manner to a game of creative footwork, exuberant teamwork and pure passion.

- There was a time in Pele's childhood when he could not even afford a football, but when his father handed him a stuffed sock, the young football-enthusiast was happy to kick it about and even went on to found a team known as 'Shoeless Ones'. In fact, the game took on his name later and became famous as 'pelada'.

- Pele composed the entire soundtrack of the 1977 biopic on him titled *Pele*.

- His 1969 visit to Nigeria resulted in a forty-eight-hour ceasefire of the civil war that was raging in the country at that time.

PETE SAMPRAS

Among the most famous tennis players of modern times, Pete Sampras is the winner of fourteen Grand Slam titles, which include seven Wimbledon championships. Nicknamed 'Pistol Pete' for his deadly first serve, Sampras was respected not only for his stamina and skill on the tennis courts but also his quiet demeanour and sober lifestyle off it.

Pete Sampras was born 12 August 1971, in Potomac, Maryland, to parents of Greek origin. However, when Pete was seven, the family moved to the warmer climes of California and the Sampras children started learning tennis. Soon, young Pete displayed an exceptional talent for the game and by the time he was twelve, he was already competing and winning against boys older than him.

When young Sampras turned fourteen, he changed his game from a predominantly baseline to serve-and-volley play. Also, long-time family friend and coach, Peter Fischer, convinced the budding tennis champion to move on from two-handed to one-handed backhand. With legendary Australian player Rod Laver as his inspiration, young Sampras further honed his serve till it turned into a deadly weapon in his arsenal of tennis moves.

Armed with his new training, Sampras turned professional in 1988 and just a couple of years later, he bagged his first Grand Slam title by beating Andre Agassi in the finals in straight sets to become the youngest winner of the US Open.

The next Grand Slam title took a while to come but the wait was well worth the sweet victory at the prestigious British centre courts in 1993, where Sampras won his first Wimbledon title. This was only the beginning of a glorious British connection during which Sampras would go on to win the Wimbledon title seven times, including four straight championships from 1997 to 2000.

In 1993, Sampras garnered his second US Open singles title and the next year, he bagged the Australian Open championship as well. Despite 1995 being a time of personal hardship for Sampras—who found that this coach and friend Tim Gullikson was fighting terminal brain cancer—he won the US Open and successfully defended this title next year too. In 1997, Sampras won the Australian Open once more and in 2002, came his last Grand Slam title with the US Open win. He was named the ATP 'Player of the Year' as well as the top ranked player for six consecutive years from 1993 to 1998.

Staying away from on-court histrionics, Sampras became the poster boy for mature sportsmanship and quiet confidence; he let his game speak for himself. Equipped with a powerful serve, strong ground-strokes and unflagging determination to win, Sampras silently made his way into the gallery of all-time tennis greats.

- Interestingly, Sampras never won a French Open title during his illustrious career.
- Sampras suffers from thalasemmia minor, a form of anaemia found in people of Mediterranean origin.

PULLELA GOPICHAND

Pullela Gopichand is among India's most famous badminton players who won the highly coveted All England Badminton Championships title in 2001. Born on 16 November 1973, at Nagandla in the Indian state of Andhra Pradesh, Gopichand, like thousands of boys in India, was keen on playing cricket during his childhood. However, on the suggestion of his brother, he switched to playing badminton around the age of eleven. After finishing school, he joined Andhra Vidyalaya College in Hyderabad in preparation for an engineering degree. In the meantime, Gopichand found himself improving at badminton till he was chosen to lead the Combined Universities team in 1990 and then again in 1991.

When in 1991 Gopichand was also selected to the state-level junior badminton team, he realized that this is what he wanted to do for the rest of his life. Despite reservations from his father, the young man quit studies to focus full-time on badminton. Gopichand proved that he made the right decision when, at the age of eighteen, he won the Junior National Championship title. However, the achievement also drove home the importance of right training and Gopichand thus shifted base from Hyderabad to Bangalore (now Bengaluru) to join the Prakash Padukone Badminton Academy run by the former Indian badminton champion.

Unfortunately, a series of knee injuries and a painful surgery in the early 1990s kept Gopichand out of action for quite some time. But such was his perseverance and passion for the sport, that in 1996 he not only returned to badminton but even went on to win the National Badminton Championships title in what would be the first of a straight series of five such titles till 2000.

In 1998, Gopichand won a bronze medal in singles at the Commonwealth Games as well as a silver medal as part of the team event. After reaching the finals of the Thomas Cup in 2000, Gopichand touched the peak of his playing career in 2001 when he defeated China's Chen Hong in straight sets to win the prestigious All England Championships title.

Though Gopichand did not win any major title after 2001, he began the next phase of his career as a coach of the Indian national badminton team in 2006. A couple of years later, he fulfilled a long cherished dream by opening his very own badminton academy to train the younger generation of badminton players. In recognition of his contribution to Indian badminton, Gopichand has been honoured by several State awards, among which are the Padma Shri in 2005 and the Padma Bhushan in 2014.

- Gopichand proved successful in his avatar as a coach as well when two of his students, Saina Nehwal and P.V. Sindhu, eventually won the bronze medal at the 2012 Summer Olympics and the silver medal at the 2016 Summer Olympics, respectively.

- Gopichand is a graduate in Public Administration from A.V. College, Hyderabad.

- He is married to P. V. V. Lakshmi–a former badminton player herself.

P.T. USHA

P.T. Usha was the first Indian woman track and field athlete to gain worldwide fame. Born as Pilavullakandi Thekkeparambil Usha on 27 June 1964, in Payyoli, a small town in Kerala, India's future sprint queen was raised in humble circumstances. Though she was a natural athlete from her childhood, the first opportunity to hone her skills came in 1976 when the state government started a sports school for women in Kannore, and Usha was selected to represent her district.

Fortunately, Usha's potential was spotted by famed Indian athletics coach O.M. Nambiar during the 1976 National School Games, and he then took over her training. Usha's talent bloomed as a result of a superior level of coaching and after a series of medals at the district and state levels, she swept the women's athletics events at the 1979 National Games as well as the National inter-state meet next year, setting many national-level records as well.

In 1980, Usha got an opportunity to go to Moscow, thus becoming the youngest Indian sprinter—male or female—to compete in an Olympic Games. She was, however, eliminated at the heats but came back more determined for the next Olympic Games. At Los Angeles, Usha became the first Indian female athlete to participate in an Olympic Games final when she got ready to compete in the 400 metre hurdles—the very first year that the event was introduced for women in the Olympics.

P.T. Usha found the greatest success in her career at the continent level. At the 1985 Asian Championships held in Jakarta, she won five gold medals and one bronze medal besides being declared the 'Best Woman Athlete' of the meet. The very next year at the Seoul Asian Games, she won the gold medal in four events and a silver in one—a stellar performance which brought her the Adidas 'Golden Shoe' award given to the best athlete of the meet. By the time she retired, Usha had one hundred and one international medals under her belt, besides holding the record for being the first Indian woman to reach the finals of any Olympic Games. In recognition of her contribution to Indian athletics, she has also been honoured by prestigious State awards, such as the Arjuna Award which is given for excellence in sports, as well as the Padma Shri in 1984. Currently, Usha runs her own sports academy near Kozhikode, Kerala, to train budding athletes and prepare them for international competitions.

- Unfortunately, in the Los Angeles Olympic Games, Usha missed out on a medal by a mere 1/100th of a second, though her time of 55.42 seconds in the 400 metre hurdles continues to be a national record.

- P.T. Usha would get a meagre stipend of ₹250 at the sports school in Kannore.

PYRROS DIMAS

Albanian-born Greek weightlifter Pyrros Dimas is famous for winning gold medals in three consecutive Olympic Games besides holding three World Championships titles and one European Championships title in the sport. With such achievements under his belt, Dimas is regarded as the most successful competitive weightlifter in modern times.

Dimas was born on 13 October 1971, in Himara, southern Albania, in a family of Greek origin. He began weightlifting as a sport when just eleven years old and by eighteen, he was the triple champion from Albania, in the 82.5 kg category. Dimas not only repeated the feat next year, but went on to sweep the 1990 European Weightlifting Championships, where he improved his world ranking from the 12th to 4th position and in the process, helped Albania reach the No.3 spot in international rankings just behind Russia and Bulgaria. This led the European Weightlifting Federation to bestow on him the title of 'European Master', while the Albanian government honoured him with the title 'Master of Sports'

In 1991, Dimas travelled to Greece—reportedly on the pretext of undergoing surgery—and promptly applied for Greek citizenship. It came through right in time for the 1992 Olympic Games and at Barcelona, Dimas won a gold medal in the 82.5 kg event. His dedication of this win, to Greece, when he shouted his famous cry, 'For Greece', became an iconic moment of the Games and prompted an outpouring of adulation for him as well as 100-metre-hurdles sprinter Voula Patoulidou, upon their return to the country.

Dimas next went on to lift the World Championship titles at Melbourne in 1993 and at Guangzhou in 1995, which was also the year of his European Championships win at Warszawa.

In 1996, Dimas was given the honour of being the flagbearer for Greece at the Atlanta Olympic Games. He lived up to his country's aspirations by not only winning a gold medal in the 83 kg category but also setting a world record for lifting a staggering 392.5 kg in total. At the 2000 Sydney Olympic Games, Dimas competed in the 85 kg clean-and-jerk event and emerged the winner. This gold medal would be his last; in 2004, he would return from Athens with a bronze medal on account of a wrist injury. Nevertheless, Dimas received a standing ovation from the audience after he announced his retirement from competitive weightlifting.

Nicknamed 'The Lion of Himara' after his Albanian birthplace, Dimas is regarded as one of the greatest athletes in the history of weightlifting. Dimas later became the President of the Hellenic Weightlifting Federation.

- Such was Dimas's physical prowess that he would continue to hold the weights above his head even after the buzzer had sounded the end of the time, so that the audience could continue clicking pictures.

- Post retirement, Dimas joined national politics and showed solidarity with the cause of Northern Epirus.

RAFAEL NADAL

Rafael Nadal is one of the most successful contemporary tennis players who has fifteen Grand Slam titles besides two Olympic gold medals under his belt.

Born in Mallorca, Spain, on June 3 1986, Nadal started playing tennis when he was just three years old. It was, in fact, his uncles Miguel Angel Nadal (who was a former professional player himself) and Toni Nadal, who spotted young Rafael's potential for the sport and began coaching him. By the time young Nadal was eight, he had won an under-12 regional tennis championship and in another four years, he claimed the Spanish as well as European Championships titles in that age category. Not surprisingly, Nadal turned professional when only fifteen.

Nadal's first international win came in 2005 when, as a nineteen-year-old, he won the French Open. He would go on to win an incredible eleven singles titles the same year, eight of which would be on clay courts. Nadal continued to defend his French Open till 2017, barring just two years—2009 and 2015.

2008 turned out to be an especially successful year for Nadal as he not only won the gold medal at the Beijing Olympic Games but went on to defeat Roger Federer at Wimbledon too. The 2008 Wimbledon singles win was particularly sweet for Nadal as it firmly established him as more than a clay-court specialist and a true tennis champion—a fact that was reflected in his ascent to the top of world tennis rankings the same year.

In 2009, Nadal added the Australian Open championship to his list of wins. The following year, by sweeping the Wimbledon, French Open and US Open, Nadal finally completed the Career Golden Slam. The highly coveted achievement includes the four major championships as well as the Olympic gold medal and in 2010, Nadal became only the second male player in the history of tennis to do so.

A knee condition kept Nadal away from 2012 Olympic Games but the very next year, he stormed back to lift the French Open Cup and later won the US Open as well—thus reclaiming the No.1 ranking as well.

In 2014, Nadal won his ninth French Open championship title but suffered an upset the next year. While 2016 saw him pull out of the tournament due to a wrist injury, he went on to win titles at Monte Carlo and Barcelona. Also, the year brought him his second Olympic gold medal when Nadal won the men's doubles event with partner Marc Lopez at the Rio Games.

With his signature top-spin heavy shots, amazing resilience and his eventual mastery of other surfaces, Nadal has made a place for himself among the modern tennis greats.

- A virtually unbeatable force on clay courts, Nadal, nicknamed 'King of Clay', has–as of 2017–won the French Open a record ten times.

- Nadal admits to being afraid of dogs, according to his 2010 autobiography, *Rafa*.

- He has appeared in a music video of Shakira's song, called 'Gypsy'.

ROD LAVER

Widely considered the greatest tennis player of the twentieth century, Rod Laver's career spanned four years before, and three years after, the beginning of the Open Era. During that time, he became the first player to achieve two calendar-year Grand Slams by winning the four major tennis championships, including the Wimbledon, the Australian Open, French Open and US Open, in the same year—a record that even after fifty years of the Open Era, no other man has been able to match.

Born as Rodney George Laver on 9 August 1938, in Rockhampton, Queensland, Australia, the future tennis icon grew up in a family of tournament lawn tennis players. Right from his childhood, Rod played with his three other siblings.

While attending a tennis camp, young Rod came into the notice of Australian Davis Cup captain, Harry Hopman, who then began training the budding tennis champion. The guidance paid off and at eighteen, young Laver was selected into the Australian Davis Cup team.

1959 proved to be the year of Laver's first major victory since he not only won the Australian doubles championship with Robert Mark but gained international attention by claiming the mixed-doubles title at the Wimbledon championships with Darlene Hard. The next year, he won the Australian singles and in 1961, the first of his four Wimbledon singles championship titles. He would also go on to win the doubles titles at the Wimbledon twice.

In 1962 came the first of Laver's Grand Slams when he won all the four major singles championships that were held in Australia, England, France and the United States. The next year, Laver turned professional and dominated the professional circuit. Between 1966 and 1970, he won nineteen straight US Pro titles.

With the start of the Open Era in 1968, Laver was back in the Grand Slam championships and the same year, he took less than an hour to vanquish his rival at the Wimbledon singles final and lift the Cup. In 1969, Laver achieved what no one till then had, or since then has, been able to do in the history of tennis—win a calendar-year Grand Slam for the second time.

Laver continued his dominance of international tennis for roughly another decade till he finally retired in 1978. In 1981, he was welcomed into the International Tennis Hall of Fame. In 2000, the centre court at Australia's Melbourne Park, which is the the main venue of the Australian Open, was named Rod Laver Court, in his honour.

However Laver's real legacy lay in the stylistic innovations that he brought about as well as the way he transformed the status of the players. Despite a relatively unremarkable physical stature, Laver demolished opponents with his left-handed top-spin strokes and introduced power into the sport. Also, he was the first professional player to top a million dollars in prize money which, together with his domination of all the Grand Slam championships, made him the first superstar of tennis. With a career straddling the amateur and Open, Laver's sporting and financial success would go on to inspire an entire generation of players such as John McEnroe and Pete Sampras.

- The Laver family had such a hold on the sport in and around Rockhampton that the junior final of the Central Queensland Championships was actually held in their own tennis court since both finalists were Laver boys.

- Laver was frequently introduced as 'the man with the copper hair but the golden touch'.

ROGER BANNISTER

British middle-distance runner Sir Roger Bannister is best known for being the first athlete to run a mile in less than 4 minutes. He was so passionate about running that despite being a medical student at the time, Bannister won the British mile championship three times, besides coming first in the Empire Championship and in the European 1,500 metre championship once each.

Born on 29 March 1929, in Harrow, England, Roger Bannister was a natural athlete. In school, he won the cross-country three years in a row, and when he was only sixteen, decided to become a runner.

However, a keen intellect saw him get through Oxford University where he started studying medicine in 1946. Even then, he tried to devote as much time possible to running, till he felt reasonably ready for the 1952 Olympics.

At Helsinki, Bannister competed in the 1,500 metre run but came 4th. Though he missed out on an Olympic medal, he still finished with a time of 3 minutes 46 seconds—a national record.

Disheartened by the Olympics outcome, Bannister, for a brief while, considered giving up running but eventually decided to train even harder. In Oxford, on the Iffley Road track, Bannister finally achieved the biggest running glory by being the first to shatter the 4 minute time barrier to complete a mile by defeating John Landy with his time of 3 minutes 59.4 seconds. The psychological feat was as important as the physical achievement and the sub-four-minute mile record turned Bannister into a sports hero overnight.

However, Landy was determined to make a comeback and merely forty-five days later in Finland, he broke Bannister's record by completing the mile run in 3 minutes 57.9 seconds, which was then rounded off to 3.58 by the IAAF. It was now only a matter of time before the fastest mile runners clashed again.

In 1954, Bannister finally bested Landy at the British Empire and Commonwealth Games in Vancouver.

After winning the 1,500 metre run, nicknamed the 'Metric Mile', at the European Championships in Bern, Switzerland, the same year, and setting yet another world record in the process with a time of 3 minutes 3.8 seconds, Bannister announced his retirement from running. He went on to complete his medical degree from Oxford University in 1963 and eventually specialized in neurology. For his sporting achievements as well as valuable research into several neurological subjects, Roger Bannister was knighted in 1975 by Queen Elizabeth II of England

- A 1954 British Empire and Commonwealth Games race, billed 'The Miracle Mile', saw John Landy leading for most of the way till in the last bend, Bannister edged past the former, and in looking back to gauge the difference, Landy fell behind Bannister, who won with a time of 3 minutes 58.8 seconds.

- Bannister once said, 'I just ran anywhere and everywhere—never because it was an end in itself, but because it was easier for me to run than to walk.'

ROGER FEDERER

Today, Swiss tennis champion Roger Federer is accepted as among the top players in the recent history of the sport. He has reigned at the top of world tennis rankings for three hundred and two weeks, which is the longest in men's tennis.

Born on 8 August 1981, in Basel, Switzerland, young Federer grew up playing tennis and soccer. But after he became one of the top three junior tennis players in his country at the age of eleven, he realized that if he wanted sports as a career, he would have to channel his energy and time on any one game. The decision paid off and at fourteen, he swept away the Swiss national junior championship title. In 1998, he made his debut at the junior Wimbledon and went on to win the boys' singles and doubles titles. At the end of the same year, Federer decided to go pro and in 1999, made his debut on the Swiss Davis Cup team.

In keeping with his quiet and steady personality, Federer's rise to the top of the sport was gradual. At the 2000 Olympic Games, he settled for a bronze medal and took another three years to make his way to his first Grand Slam title—the 2003 Wimbledon singles title which would be the first of a total of eight on the prestigious grass court.

Like a true genius of the sport, Federer plays well on other surfaces too. He has won five US Open singles titles, six Australian Open singles titles, eight Wimbledon titles and the 2009 French Open singles title. To a great extent, his long and varied reign in the world of tennis owes to his versatile technique. Apart from lightning speed aces and a powerful forehand, he is adept in elements such as backhand smash, jump smash, sky-hook and half-volley. In times when professional tennis is driven mainly by power and physical strength, Federer's fluid style and graceful shots are a delight to fans all over the world.

- With twenty Grand Slam singles titles under his belt, Federer holds the record for the maximum number of such titles in the world held by a male tennis player.

- Two days after winning his first Wimbledon, Federer received from the Swiss tournament organizers a 1,760-lb milking cow as a gift that he went on to name, 'Juliette'.

SACHIN TENDULKAR

Indian cricketer Sachin Tendulkar is considered among the greatest batsmen in the history of the sport. In an international career that spanned two decades, he broke and set several world records such as being the only batsman to score hundred international centuries and complete 30,000 runs in international cricket. As of November 2017, even after four years of his retirement in 2013, Tendulkar remains the maximum scorer of runs in both ODI as well as Test cricket.

Born on 24 April 1973, in Mumbai—then known as Bombay—the commercial capital of India, Tendulkar grew up in a middle-class family. Since childhood, young Tendulkar was passionate about cricket. The family's move to a neighbourhood near Shivaji Park Stadium meant that the budding cricketer could not only practise longer but also came into the notice of cricket coach Ramakant Achrekar, who began training him. All the hard work paid off when he was selected for the Indian national team in 1989.

Tendulkar came into his own in the 1990 tour of England where his 119-run knock not only pulled back India from defeat but also made him the second-youngest player to make a century in Test cricket. A double-century against Australia in 1992 paved the way for Tendulkar being invited to play for the Yorkshire Club—the first international player to do so.

Tendulkar's phenomenal success as a batsman led him to don the captain's mantle in 1996 but the additional responsibilities proved too much for the twenty-three-year-old. His batting suffered along with the performance of the Indian team. In 1998, relieved of captaincy, Tendulkar rose to the peak of his batting career. In March 2001, Tendulkar became the first batsman to score 10,000 runs in ODI cricket while playing a five-match series against Australia. The very next year, he reached another cricket milestone with his thirtieth Test century, thus breaking Don Bradman's record of twenty-nine. Though India lost to Australia in the 2003 World Cup, Tendulkar turned out to be the leading scorer, for which he was presented with the 'Man of the Series' award.

After 2003, however, Tendulkar's batting was bogged down by a series of injuries and negative public feedback. He recovered in 2007 to deliver a power-packed performance against Bangladesh in a Test series and then against England and Australia in the ODI series. In 2011, driven chiefly by his batting prowess, India won the World Cup and the next year, he attained his 100th international century. Soon after, Tendulkar announced his retirement from ODI cricket and after a year, he exited from all formats of the sport, including the Indian Premier League (IPL), in which he had played on the Mumbai Indians team since 2008.

Tendulkar's immense professional and financial success made him a household name in India. In a country where cricket is followed with religious fervour, he was its reigning deity for around two decades. Even now, Tendulkar continues to hold significant records, affirming his status as an all-time cricket icon.

- When as a sixteen-year-old, Tendulkar was selected for the Indian national team in 1989 that was to play a Test series against Pakistan, his father had to sign the contract papers on his behalf because he was not yet officially an adult!

- As a thirteen-year-old, Sachin once fielded for Pakistan at an exhibition match, ahead of the 1987 Test Series, since Imran Khan's team was short on fielders.

SERENA WILLIAMS

Serena Williams is an American professional tennis player who, till 2017, had won twenty-three Grand Slam singles titles—the maximum by any player, male or female—in the Open Era and continued to be the top-ranked women's tennis player in the world on eight occasions between 2002 and 2017.

Born on 26 September 1981, in Saginaw, Michigan, Serena was the youngest in a family of five daughters. Her father, though a former sharecropper from Louisiana, helped two of his youngest daughters learn the basics of tennis on public courts of Los Angeles. Serena, as well as her older sister Venus, soon became skilled in the sport.

In 1995, Serena turned professional, though it would be another four years before she would win her first Grand Slam tournament in 1999 at the US Open. A period of indifferent play followed till she rebounded in 2002 to win the French Open, the US Open and the Wimbledon. With the Australian Open championship title under her belt next year and thus having won all the four major tournament titles, Serena achieved a career Grand Slam in 2003 and went on to reaffirm her dominance in women's tennis by seizing the Wimbledon singles championship title the same year too.

Beset by nagging injuries, Serena had to lie low for a while but stormed back in 2007 with her third Australian Open championship title which increased to five in 2010—the year that saw her winning her third Wimbledon title as well.

After yet another break caused by health-related issues, Serena returned stronger than ever and won the gold medal in the singles category at the 2012 Olympics—thus becoming the second female tennis player after Steffi Graf to achieve a Golden Slam.

Since then, barring a brief phase in 2016, Serena has continued with her winning spree and in 2017, with her Australian Open singles win, she amassed an incredible twenty-three Grand Slam singles titles—the most held by any player since 1968 when the Open era in tennis began. Serena also has four Olympic gold medals—three along with Venus from doubles wins (2000, 2008 and 2012) and one in singles (2012 London Olympic Games).

Off the courts, Serena is involved in a series of ventures, ranging from giving voice in animation films, to founding a charitable organization known as the Serena Williams Foundation, which offers schooling opportunities to underprivileged children in different parts of the world. Married to billionaire and Reddit co-founder, Alexis Ohanian, Serena gave birth to their baby daughter on 1 September 2017. Considering the physical tenacity and power play that have been the hallmarks of her game, not many were surprised when the tennis star came back in March 2018, after a fourteen-month break, to win her first single match of the BNP Paribas Open in California.

- Serena has a popular clothing line titled Aneres, which is actually a reverse spelling of her name.
- Serena Williams doesn't celebrate birthdays since she is a member of the religious group, Jehovah's Witnesses.

SHANE WARNE

Australian cricketer Shane Warne was one of the greatest bowlers of modern times and became especially famous for his lethal array of leg spin dismissals. By the time he retired, Warne had racked up a Test cricket average of 25, with 708 wickets from one hundred and forty five Tests.

Born on 13 September 1969, in Ferntree Gully, in the Australian province of Victoria, young Warne was a sports enthusiast right from the beginning, playing both cricket and Australian-rules football in school. It was only after the end of the Victoria football season in 1988 that Warne decided to focus specifically on cricket.

Warne's rise on the cricket field was rapid. From playing for the Sheffield Shield domestic club competition, he quickly moved on to playing first-class cricket for the first time in February 1991 and then made his international debut the same year in September as part of the Australia B team touring Zimbabwe.

In January 1992, Warne was finally inducted into the main Australian team as it clashed with India at the Sydney Cricket Ground. However, his form remained unimpressive till August that year when he stunned the audience by taking the last 3 wickets in the second innings against Sri Lanka, without conceding a single run. Despite this glimpse of brilliance, Warne would have to wait for the second Test against West Indies before he could again prove his bowling genius with a haul of 7 wickets for just 52 runs—a performance which helped the Australians win the Boxing Day Test.

The 1993 Ashes tour turned out to be extremely successful for Warne as the six tests gave him 34 wickets at an average of 25.79. In fact, the first ball in the series—bowled to experienced English batsman Mike Gatting—went down in cricket history as the perfect specimen of a leg spinner's skill as it pitched on the leg stump but then spun menacingly past the bat to strike Gatting's off stump.

In the 1994–95 Ashes series, Warne again played brilliantly, taking 27 wickets to post an incredible average of 20.33. He not only achieved a hat trick—3 wickets on three successive balls—in the second Test of the series but his stellar 8 for 71 in the second innings of the first Test actually won the match for Australia.

A period of controversy followed as Warne was accused of taking bribes in 1998 and then tested positive for a banned substance. This even led to him being banned for a year. However, after his return, Warne went on to reach important milestones, such as taking his five-hundredth Test wicket in March 2004; becoming the first bowler in August 2005 while playing the third Ashes Test to take 600 wickets; breaking the record for the maximum number of wickets in a calendar year with 96 wickets; and finally posting an incredible average of 19.92 in the 2005 Ashes series, where he not only took 40 wickets but also scored 249 runs..

In 2007, Warne decided to retire from Test cricket and after a successful tenure with Rajasthan Royals in the IPL, finally called it a day in 2011. He continues to display his passion for cricket as a popular TV commentator and has recently taken up professional poker.

- An indication of Warne's contribution to cricket, especially in the art of leg-spin bowling was his selection, in 2000, among the five 'Wisden Cricketers of the Century' and most importantly, his position as the only specialist bowler in the hallowed group.

- Of his achievement, Warne once said, '400 wickets is four hundred more than I thought I'd get.'

SHAUN WHITE

Shaun White is an American professional snowboarder and skateboarder. The winner of two gold medals at the 2006 and 2010 Winter Olympic Games, White has several medals from extreme sports events—such as X Games and Winter X Games—under his belt.

White was born on 3 September 1986, in San Diego, California. Young Shaun was influenced by his older brother Jesse, and took up skateboarding. By the time he was six, Shaun had started snowboarding and eventually started practising in smaller ski resorts such as Bear Mountain and Okema Mountain that dot southern California.

When he was nine, young Shaun was spotted practising at a local skate park by famous professional skateboarder Tony Hawk. Hawk then guided him through the paces of the sport till White felt confident enough to go professional at seventeen. Eventually, he would go on to win two X Games gold medals in the vert event, in 2007 and 2011, besides bagging the overall title of 'Action Sports Tour Champion'

It was snowboarding though that brought White, international fame. He started competing in the Winter X Games in 2002 and, since then, won a medal every year till 2013. In fact, he set a world record by being the first male snowboarder to achieve a four-peat in a single event—the slopestyle. A greater glory came White's way when he won the gold medals in the men's halfpipe at the

2006 Winter Olympics held in Turin, Italy, and then defended his title four years later in the Vancouver Winter Olympics.

In 2012, White suffered negative press after he was arrested for vandalism and public intoxication during a hotel stay in Tennessee. Professionally too, White's career took a dip, as during the 2014 Winter Olympic Games, he failed to win any medal in Sochi, Russia.

However, White still remains the most popular professional snowboarder. Nicknamed the 'Flying Tomato' because of his shock of red hair, White has long attracted major sponsors such as Target, Mountain Dew, T-mobile and Hewlett Packard. In recent times, he has multiplied his financial success with his own apparel brand, snowboarding video games as well as several snowboarding DVDs.

- A congenital heart defect made White go through two open heart surgeries–even before he had turned one.
- White was a central protagonist in a documentary on snowboarders, called *First Descent*. It was released in 2006.

STEFFI GRAF

Former German tennis pro Steffi Graf became one of the most successful female tennis players of the Open era. With her killer forehand and single-minded focus on the game, she dominated women's tennis for a decade—from the mid-1980s to 1990s. By the time she retired in 1999, Graf had amassed an incredible twenty-two Grand Slam singles titles including a Golden Slam in 1988 when she not only won all the four major championships—the French Open, the Australian Open, the US Open and Wimbledon—but an Olympic gold medal as well.

Born as Stephanie Maria Graf on 14 June 1969, in Mannheim, West Germany, the future tennis champion was an early inductee into the sport. When she was only four, she was gifted a tennis racquet by her father—a national-level player himself—and just two years later, she won her first junior tournament.

Graf's father continued to coach her, and soon it became clear that she was one of the brightest rising stars in the world of tennis. Graf went on to win not only the 14-and-under and 18-and-under championships in her country but the Orange Bowl in Florida as well—all before she even turned fourteen.

In October 1982, Graf—then only thirteen years and four months of age—turned professional and a few weeks later, became the second-youngest player in the history of the sport to attain an international ranking. In 1984, tennis, during the Olympic Games, was still a demonstration sport but Graf easily outplayed everyone else to win an honorary gold medal.

Graf's first Grand Slam title came in 1987 when she defeated then reigning tennis powerhouse Martina Navratilova to lift the French Open women's singles shield. Next year brought the crowning glory of her career when she won all the four women's singles Grand Slam championship titles and also the gold medal in the Seoul Olympic Games, thus attaining the Golden Grand Slam of her career.

Graf's winning spree saw her setting the record for being the youngest woman to reach five hundred career wins in October 1991. The next year in the Atlanta Olympics though, she had to settle for a silver medal. This was also a period of personal tumult in Graf's life as her father was convicted and imprisoned for financial fraud. Such incidents took their toll, and by the end of the 1990s, Graf was beset with nagging injuries, despite which she went on to win the French Open in 1999 and gave a tough fight in the Wimbledon's final that year. However, with the realization that she was enjoying tennis lesser with every match, Graf announced her retirement in August 1999. In 2004, she was welcomed into the International Tennis Hall of Fame.

Post-retirement, Graf married American tennis champion, Andre Agassi, in October 2001 and welcomed their first child. Currently, Graf remains busy with raising her two kids, promoting her line of fashion accessories as well as her charity, titled Children for Tomorrow, which she founded to help children in crisis-hit parts of the world.

- In 1993, a mentally-ill, self-acclaimed Graf fan stabbed Monica Seles, her primary competitor at that time, though Graf herself was completely exonerated.

- In 1986, Graf was the subject of a song titled, 'I am in love with Stefi Graf', sung by Hugh Laurie on his show, *A Bit of Fry and Laurie*.

STEVE REDGRAVE

Sir Steve Redgrave is perhaps the most widely recognized name in competitive rowing across the world. A five-time gold medallist in five straight Olympic Games as well as a nine-time winner of the World Rowing Championships title, Redgrave also holds the record for remaining undefeated in four consecutive seasons.

Redgrave was born on 23 March 1962, in Barlow, England, in a modest working-class family. However, he soon discovered a passion for rowing which opened up an avenue for success.

Redgrave made his Olympic debut in 1984 at Los Angeles where he promptly won a gold medal at the coxed four race. Four years later, he partnered with Andrew Holmes to bring back the gold medal for coxless pairs as well as the bronze medal for the coxswain race from Seoul Olympics. At the 1992 Barcelona Olympic Games, Redgrave teamed up with a new mate, Matthew Pinset, and again won the gold medal in coxless pairs. The duo went on to win the gold medal at the 1996 Olympics too, though Redgrave returned from Atlanta emotionally and physically drained.

However, it was not long before Redgrave was back to training with his sights firmly set on the next Olympic Games to be held in Sydney in 2000. Redgrave realized that this would be his toughest challenge since he was not only battling health issues such as diabetes but by the time 2000 rolled in, he would be past thirty-six. Nevertheless, his endurance and skill brought

Redgrave his fifth consecutive Olympic gold medal when he, along with fellow British rowers Pinsent, Jim Cracknell and Tim Foster, won the coxless four.

Redgrave has been equally successful in other tournaments. He has won the World Rowing Championships a staggering nine times starting from 1986. Besides that, he has won three Commonwealth Games gold medals—all in 1986. Again, Redgrave has been a familiar face at Henley Royal Regatta for over two decades, with several wins in tournaments such as the Silver Goblets & Nickalls' Challenge Cup, Stewards' Challenge Cup, the Queen Mother Challenge Cup, and the like. In recognition of his long successful career in competitive rowing, Redgrave was knighted in 2001 and awarded the BBC Sports 'Lifetime Achievement Award' in 2011.

- Young Redgrave could not finish schooling since he was dyslexic and found it difficult to cope with the academic curriculum.

- He is married to a fellow Olympic rower by the name of Ann Callaway.

SUNIL GAVASKAR

Considered one of the best opening batsmen in the history of cricket, former Indian player Sunil Gavaskar dominated the sport in the 1970s and '80s. He was the first cricketer to score 10,000 runs in Test cricket and over his sixteen-year career, set various records which remained unbroken for many decades. By the time Gavaskar retired, he had an envious Test batting average of 51.12 runs.

Sunil Gavaskar was born on 10 July 1949, in Mumbai. Influenced by his maternal uncle Madhav Mantri, a Test player himself, young Sunil trained earnestly till he made it to the Vazir Sultan Colts XI, thus marking his entry into first-class cricket.

Gavaskar's international debut followed with the 1970–71 tour of West Indies where he racked up a staggering total of 774 runs, thus helping India clinch the series. He returned home to find himself hailed as a national hero who was often expected to amass massive totals, and Gavaskar managed to fulfil them most of the time, such as the 1977–78 tour of Australia when he scored three consecutive Test centuries in the first three tests as well as the 1985–86 tour of Australia in which he remained unbeaten at 166 in the first Test and at 172 in the third Test. Gavaskar was also part of the Indian cricket team that won the 1983 World Cup in England.

Unlike his role of the opening batsman, Gavaskar did not turn out to be a very successful captain. Twice, he was made to lead the national cricket team but both times, he was eventually replaced by Kapil Dev, then the leading medium-pace bowler of India.

Nevertheless, Gavaskar kept racking up huge scores in his matches. He beat Sir Donald Bradman's record of twenty-nine Test centuries and at one time, held the record for making the maximum number of Test runs and Test centuries in the world. Gavaskar was also the only Test batsman from India to have made two centuries on three occasions. Additionally, he was a skilled fielder who took one hundred and eight catches during his career. Gavaskar's achievements have inspired generations of youngsters in cricket-crazy India—including another legend, Sachin Tendulkar, who, on the occasion of India's five-hundredth Test match revealed that he would have loved to played alongside 'Sunil Sir' who figures among his 'cricketing heroes'. Gavaskar retired after the 1987 World Cup and continues to enjoy a successful run as a cricket commentator in the electronic and print media. In 2009, he was inducted into the International Cricket Council's Hall of Fame.

- Gavaskar was nicknamed 'Little Master' for his five-feet-five-inch height.
- During the Hindu-Muslim riots of 1992-93 in Mumbai, Gavaskar saved a family by standing between them and a raging mob.

SANIA MIRZA

The best-known female tennis player in India, Sania Mirza figures among the most successful doubles tennis players in the world as well. As of October 2017, she has won three Grand Slam doubles and another three Grand Slam mixed-doubles titles. In 2015, she even reached the top of WTA women's doubles rankings.

Born on 15 November 1986 in the bustling metropolis of Mumbai, Sania soon moved with her family to Hyderabad. Here she began learning from her father right from the age of six. Despite enrolling in St. Mary's College, Sania was determined to take up tennis as a profession.

From 2001 onwards, Mirza started competing in the International Tennis Federation (ITF) tournaments and soon proved herself as a promising player in the junior tennis circuit, where she won ten singles and thirteen doubles titles in all. The highlight of this phase was the Wimbledon's girls' doubles championship title that she won with her partner Alisa Kleybanova in 2003. The same year, she also won the US Open girls' doubles semi-finals, besides bagging four gold medals in the Afro-Asian games held in her home city, Hyderabad.

In 2005, Mirza was judged the WTA 'Newcomer of the Year' on the basis of her consistent efforts at Grand Slam singles tournaments. However, a wrist injury in 2008 forced her out of action for around a year. The next year, Mirza decided to make a comeback as a doubles player so as to go easy on her wrist. The choice turned out to be the right one as she went on to win the Australian Open mixed-doubles in 2009 with Mahesh Bhupathi and three years later, the duo lifted the same title at the French Open as well. In 2014, Mirza would bag another Grand Slam mixed-doubles title—this time with Bruno Soares at the US Open.

In the meantime though, Mirza kept struggling with persistent injuries and inconsistent play. After a series of doubles partners, she finally found her rhythm with Swiss player Martina Hingis and the two went on to win the Wimbledon's women's doubles title in 2015. This was Mirza's first Grand Slam win in women's doubles and she continued with the partnership which proved extremely successful for the rest of the year. Mirza and Hingis closed 2015 by winning the women's doubles title in the WTA as well as the US Open tournaments. The same year, Mirza reached the top of WTA women's doubles rankings, which affirmed her position as the best female doubles tennis player in the world in 2015.

Mirza and Hingis seemed poised to continue their winning spree in 2016, when they emerged victorious in the Australian Open women's doubles championship—but split later in the year. Despite a few losses, Mirza ended 2016 as the year-end No.1 female doubles player—for the second time in a row.

Armed with a powerful forehand and superb groundstrokes, Mirza has emerged as the most successful female tennis player in India, besides being a world-class doubles player. For her contribution to Indian tennis, she has been awarded State awards, such as the Padma Shri (2006) and the Padma Vibhushan (2016), and has been named among the 100 Most Influential People of the World in 2016 by *Time*.

- Mirza's official biography is titled *Ace Against Odds* and was published in 2016.

- Sania Mirza is married to Pakistani cricketer Shoaib Malik and despite the two countries being arch-rivals in sports, she continues to represent India in tennis.

SERGEY BUBKA

Sergey Bubka is a name taken in the same breath as pole vault—the sport that he popularized across the world. Bubka was the first pole vaulter to clear the 6 metre and also the 6.10 metre mark.

Bubka was born on 14 December 1963, in Voroshilovgrad, a town in erstwhile Soviet Union but which is now the Ukrainian city of Luhansk. A keen athlete since childhood, young Bubka was especially fascinated by pole vaulting and was able to hone his skills under the guidance of famous coach, Vitaly Petrov. Though Bubka made his international debut at the 1981 European Junior Championship, he finished 7th. However, just two years later, at the 1983 world track and field championships held at Helsinki, he stunned the world by seizing the gold medal with a height of 5.70 metres.

Bubka then moved from strength to strength, setting new pole vault world records at every track and field meet. The first of these came on 26 May 1984 when he cleared 5.85 metres and barely a year later on 13 July 1985, achieved what was considered the ultimate target by vaulters in those times—a height of 6 metres that he crossed at an international athletics meet in Paris. In a span of four years—from 1984 to 1988—Bubka raised the world record by 21 cm which was more than what pole vaulters had been able to achieve in the past twelve years.

At the Olympic Games though, Bubka's record-breaking spree slowed down. The only time he won an Olympic gold medal was at Seoul in 1988, where he went on to set a new Olympic record of 5.9 metres. The following Olympics gave him no more opportunity to set new records even though he would continue to scale new heights in the early 1990s. For example, in 1991, at San Sebastian, Spain, he became the first pole vaulter to cross 6.1 metres and then in 1994, he vaulted over 6.14 metres—a record that remains untouched till today.

However, Bubka's inability to qualify for the 2000 Sydney Olympics made him announce his retirement the next year. He was soon invited by the IAAF to serve in an administrative capacity even as he was working with the Ukrainian government to guide budding athletes in his country of origin. Bubka has also served in the IOC and continues to be a valuable member. Yet Bubka's real legacy has been the unimaginable heights to which he pushed the sport of pole vaulting. His technique came to be known as the Bubka/Petrov model. This technique depended upon a combination of strength, agility and sheer speed, and it not only brought about valuable innovations to the sport but also enabled him to set more world records than anyone in the history of pole vaulting.

- In a career that lasted eighteen years, Bubka broke the world record an incredible thirty-five times and in fact, bested his own performance as many as fourteen times.

- Though his name is virtually synonymous with pole vault now, Bubka began his sporting career as an athlete, running sprints and long jumps.

SUSHIL KUMAR

Sushil Kumar is an Olympic-medal-winning, Indian freestyle wrestling champion. By winning a bronze medal in the 2008 Olympics and a silver medal in the 2012 Olympics, he became the first Indian to win individual medals in consecutive Olympic Games.

Born on 26 May 1983 in Baprola village, which lies near the state border between Delhi and Haryana in northern India, Kumar joined the traditional Indian wrestling school, known as akhara, when he was only fourteen years old.

Sushil Kumar's first international victory came in 2000 when he won a gold medal at the Asian Junior Wrestling Championships. From 2003, he started competing in the men's championships and went on to win the gold in the 60 kg category at the Commonwealth Wrestling Championships held at London the same year as well as the bronze medal in the 2003 Asian Championships.

The 2005 Commonwealth Championships held at Cape Town turned out to be more successful since he won two medals—a gold in the 66 kg freestyle and a bronze in the 66 kg Greco-Roman categories. In 2007, he defended his Commonwealth gold medal besides winning a silver medal in the Asian Championships held at Bishkek.

In 2008, Kumar won the bronze medal at the Asian Championships held at Jeju Island but even more importantly, gained worldwide recognition with his bronze medal at the 2008 Olympic Games in Beijing. This was the beginning of the best phase of his career as he went on to bag gold medals at the 2009 Commonwealth Championships at Jalandhar, the 2010 Asian Championships and Commonwealth Games held in New Delhi, and the Moscow World Championship in the same year.

The London Olympics of 2012 saw Kumar winning the silver medal in the 66 kg freestyle event but two years later, he confidently returned from Glasgow with the gold in the 74 kg freestyle category at the 2014 Commonwealth Games.

With so many wins at international wrestling tournaments, Sushil Kumar has gained a superstar status in the sport in India. In 2009, the Indian Government honoured him with the Rajiv Gandhi Khel Ratna.

- Interestingly, though wrestlers are required to bulk up, Sushil Kumar is a strict vegetarian and has always avoided meat products to achieve the same.

- His father was a Delhi Transport Corporation (DTC) bus driver but always supported his son's sporting dreams.

SAINA NEHWAL

One of the most successful sportspersons in India, Saina Nehwal is a professional female singles badminton champion. A former World No.1 player, she is the winner of the 2012 Olympics bronze medal besides ten badminton BWF Super Series championship titles.

Born on 17 March 1990 in the north Indian town of Hissar, Haryana, Saina moved with her family to the southern metropolis of Hyderabad after a few years. Here began her love affair with badminton and she was initially coached by Nani Prasad. Soon though, she caught the attention of award-winning badminton coach, S.M. Arif, who started training her for the international circuit. Later, she would be coached by former badminton champion Pullela Gopichand as well.

The specialized training paid off and in 2006, Nehwal won the under-19 national championships. And yet this was just the beginning of her numerous sports milestones. Twice, she won the Asian Satellite Badminton Tournament (India Chapter)—setting a record for being the only Indian player to do so. Even more importantly, she won a 4-star tournament—the Philippines Open—in 2006, thus making history by being the only female player from India and the youngest in Asia to achieve the feat.

In 2008, Nehwal won the gold medal by sweeping away all competition in the girls' singles category at the World Junior Badminton Championships. Though she could not progress beyond the quarter-finals at the Beijing Olympics held the same year, she seized the gold medal at the 2008 Chinese Taipei Open. Next year, upon acing the Indonesian Open, she became the first Indian to win a BWF Super Series title. Also in 2009, she won the Singapore Open Super Series, thus proving to the world that she was no ephemeral talent.

At the Commonwealth Games held in New Delhi in 2010, Nehwal sent the home crowd in raptures by seizing the gold medal in the women's singles category and later went on to end the year by confidently defending her Indonesian Super Series title as well.

Nehwal's next moment of international glory came in 2012 when she brought back the bronze medal from London Olympics, to India. A wave of adulation followed and overnight, she became a role model for thousands of girls in her country.

In 2014, Nehwal won the women's singles tournament at the Australian Super Series and the following year, she emerged victorious at the India Open Grand Prix Gold after beating Spanish player Carolina Marina in a tough final. Though Marina avenged the defeat at the All England Badminton Open Championships by outplaying Nehwal in the finals, the fiery Indian came back later and at the India Open BWF Super Series defeated Marina again. The victory finally catapulted Nehwal to the top of women's BWF rankings.

In recognition of her contribution to Indian sports, and badminton in particular, in 2010 the Government of India honoured Nehwal with the Rajiv Gandhi Khel Ratna and in 2016, with the Padma Bhushan.

- Nehwal was a brown belt in karate at the time of her victory in the under-19 National Championships.
- Nehwal captained the Hyderabad Hotshots in the Indian Badminton League from 2013 to 2015.

TIGER WOODS

One of the most successful names in the history of professional golf, Tiger Woods has been awarded the PGA 'Player of the Year' title an incredible ten times. In 1997, he became the youngest golfer and first player of non-white descent to win the highly coveted Masters tournament and eventually went on to add another thirteen major tournament titles to his name.

Born as Eldrick Tont Woods, on 30 December 1975, in Cypress, California, the future golfing champion was born into a mixed-race family. Not surprisingly, a fifteen-year-old Woods became the youngest winner of the US Junior Amateur Championship in 1991—a title he would go on to defend for the next two years.

After winning the United States Amateur Championship title as well, for three straight years, Woods turned professional in 1996. The very next year, he stunned the crowds at Augusta, Georgia—the venue of the Masters Tournament—by delivering a powerful game. Shooting a record 270 over 72 holes, he became the youngest male golfer and the first player of African ancestry to win the title.

Woods continued to dominate the professional golf circuit for the rest of the decade. In 2000, with his victory at the British Open, he set another world record by being the youngest to win all the four major tournaments, namely the US Open, the Masters, the British Open and the PGA Championship—thus achieving the Grand Slam of professional golf.

Woods continued with his winning spree for most of the 2000s—by 2007 he had won his thirteenth major golf championship title. Despite a knee surgery in 2008, Woods seized his third US Open championship title that year and with it, posted his career's third Grand Slam—an achievement shared only by one other golfer, the legendary Jack Nicklaus.

However, 2009 brought a series of woes for Woods—both on the professional and personal fronts. He could not win any major titles that year; worse still, his marriage to Swedish model Elin Nordegren came apart in the wake of infidelity accusations. The two were finally divorced in 2010.

It would be at least another two years before Woods would find his form again. By winning the Arnold Palmer Invitational for the eighth time in 2013, he once again regained the top world ranking in professional golf.

The victory though was short-lived and from 2014 onwards, Woods was unable to win any major tournament title. A series of health issues—including four back surgeries starting from 2014 till the most recent one in April 2017—has made him lie low, since.

Despite the recent ups and downs, Tiger Woods remains one of the most successful professional golfers of all times. The winner of PGA 'Player of the Year' for a record eleven times, he—as of August 2017—still has the distinction of reigning as the World No.1 for the maximum number of consecutive (281) and total (683) weeks.

- When just three years old, Woods shot an unbelievable 48 over 9 holes, marking the arrival of a golfing prodigy on the world stage.

- On the final round of every tournament, Woods wears a red shirt, as, according to his mother, it is a 'power colour' for him.

USAIN BOLT

Described as 'the fastest man alive', Usain Bolt is a Jamaican sprinter who boasts of a tally of nine Olympic medals. Apart from setting several new records in the 100 metre and 200 metre races, he is also the only person—as of 2017—to win the gold medal in these two events over three consecutive Olympic Games—in 2008, 2012 and 2016.

Born on 21 August 1986, in Montego Bay, Jamaica, Usain Bolt grew up playing cricket and football. However, noticing the boy's innate ability to run at lightning speed, coaches at school encouraged young Bolt to focus on track and field.

Bolt's first major victory came in 2002 where, as a mere fifteen-year-old, he won the 200 metre dash at the World Junior Championship in Kingston, Jamaica, thus becoming the youngest junior champion to win a gold medal at a world tournament. Over the next few years, Bolt would be plagued by nagging injuries and lack of consistency. In 2007, however, he resurfaced at the international athletics scene with a haul of two silver medals at the World Championship in Osaka, Japan.

At the 2008 Olympic Games in Beijing, Bolt swept away all competition in the 100 and 200 metre races. He not only won gold medals in each event but set three world records as well. Four years later, at the London Olympic Games, Bolt easily defended both his 100 and 200 metre gold medals, besides setting a new Olympic time limit of 9.63 seconds in the former.

Bolt, in fact, was on such a roll that in London, he became the first sportsperson to break three world records in a single Olympic Games competition.

Not surprisingly, Bolt was the favourite in Rio de Janeiro to seize the 100 and 200 metre gold medals once again. Sure enough, he did not disappoint and added another gold medal from 4×100 metre relay to bring his 2016 Olympic gold medal tally to three. With this, Bolt set yet another record for being the first and only sportsperson to win gold medals from two individual sprints over the course of three consecutive Olympic Games.

Apart from the Olympics, Bolt has also dominated the World Championships from 2009 when he won a staggering five gold medals at the meet held in Berlin. At the 2011 World Championship, Bolt garnered three gold medals and two years later at Moscow, he increased his tally to four. Though at the 2014 Commonwealth Games, he had to be satisfied with a single gold, the very next year, he won three gold medals at the World Championship held in Beijing.

2017 proved to be less than successful for Bolt. After suffering a hamstring injury at the 2017 World Championship, he had to be content with a bronze medal. Also, with Jamaican sprinter Nesta Carter being charged with taking a banned substance, the entire team's 2008 relay win was cancelled and Bolt too, had to return his gold medal. In August 2017, Bolt announced his retirement from competitive sprint.

Along with many other world records, his personal best of 9.58 seconds and 19.19 seconds continues to be the fastest time for 100 as well as 200 metre events, as of September 2017. For his stupendous achievements, Bolt has been honoured with the IAAF 'World Athlete of the Year' six times as well as the Laureus 'Sports Personality of the Year' four times.

- Nicknamed 'Lightning Bolt', the Jamaican sprinter is widely acknowledged as the fastest runner of all times.
- In 2008, Bolt ran his second 100 metre world-record-making race with the laces of his shoes untied!

VALENTINO ROSSI

Valentino Rossi is widely recognized as the most successful professional motorcycle racers in the world today. He is a nine-time winner of Grand Prix World Championships, including a record seven-time winner of the premier class. With eighty-nine wins, Rossi also holds the all-time record for the maximum number of victories in the history of the 500 cc MotoGP racing.

Born on 16 February 1979, in Urbino, Marche, Valentino grew up watching his father race bikes professionally.

Young Rossi soon began competing in national karting championships after which he entered minimoto racing. His first notable victory came in his second season at the Italian Sport Production where he won the Italian title. The win gave him the confidence to move on to the faster pace of 125 cc racing and in 1994, he joined the Aprilia team. Two years later, he made his World Championships debut though the season ended with mixed results. In 1997, however, Rossi won eleven of the fifteen races, thereby announcing the arrival of a star on the international stage of motorcycle racing.

Sure enough in 1998, Rossi blazed to the second ranking in the 250 cc season and the very next year, he seized the World Championship title and finished the season with five pole positions and nine wins. He defended his 250 cc World Championship title with ease in 2000, fuelled his ambition to move on to the

500 cc motorcycle racing.

The opportunity came when Rossi was roped into the Honda team. In 2001, he won his first 500 cc World Championship. He finished the season with eleven wins and even went on to win the Suzuka 8 Hours Endurance Race with American partner Colin Edwards—thus becoming the first Italian to do so.

The year 2002 marked the beginning of the MotoGP bike racing era and Rossi promptly won his first race at Suzuka. At Rio de Janeiro, he won his second World Championship title and again won the next year at Malaysia. In 2003, came one of his most spectacular wins when at the Australian Grand Prix at Phillip Island, he overcame a ten-second penalty to finish first.

Rossi switched to Yamaha for the 2004 season which he kick-started with a victory at Welkom in South Africa. Once again, he won the World Championship and finished the season at the top of the world rankings with 304 points. Rossi would go on to win the World Championships for the seventh time in 2005 which would also mark his fifth consecutive title.

In 2007, Rossi ventured into the 800 cc motorcycle racing circuit and the next year, at Motegi, he seized his first 800cc MotoGP victory—thus winning his eighth overall title and sixth in the premium category. 2009 brought Rossi his ninth World Championship title besides the hundredth victory of his motorcycle racing career when he blazed ahead of competitors at the 2009 Dutch TT in Assen.

For two seasons, Rossi joined the Ducati team but then returned to Yamaha for the 2013 season. Till November 2017, he has garnered eighty-nine wins in the 500 cc MotoGP race circuit, which places Rossi at the top of its all-time rankings.

- Because of his mother's concern regarding speeding, young Rossi was encouraged to try out karting instead and even then, so insistent was the child on speed that his father had to upgrade a 60 cc kart motor to 100 cc–all this when Valentino was just five years old!

- When he races, Rossi wears the Number 46–just like his father did.

- Rossi's favourite pop band is Pink Floyd.

VIJENDER SINGH

Vijender Singh is a professional boxer from India. He is best known for getting India its first Olympic medal in boxing when he returned from Beijing in 2008 with the bronze medal in the middleweight category.

Born on 29 October 1985, in Kaluwas, a village in Haryana, Vijender Singh grew up in modest circumstances. His elder brother, Manoj, was a boxing enthusiast and it was because of him that young Vijender too got interested in the sport. While Manoj could not make time to pursue boxing after joining the Indian army, Vijender's innate talent for the sport was spotted by Jagdish Singh, a former national-level boxer himself. Soon Vijender started training under Singh at the Bhiwani Boxing Club.

In 2000 came Vijender's first major win as he won the gold medal at the Nationals. Three years later, he tasted international success by winning the silver medal at the Afro-Asian Games held in Hyderabad. At the 2006 Melbourne Commonwealth Games, Vijender reached the finals but eventually had to be satisfied with a silver medal.

The defeat at Melbourne prompted a change in category and Vijender moved from welterweight to middleweight at the 2006 Asian Games. Though he had to settle for the bronze at Doha, Qatar, he realized this was the apt category for him and he began training more intensely. The decision proved right when at the Asian Championships held next year, Vijender won the silver medal.

The highest point in Vijender's amateur boxing career came in 2008 when he returned from the Beijing Olympics with the bronze medal in the middleweight category. This made him the first Indian to win an Olympic medal in boxing. In 2009, Vijender won bronze medals at the World Championships held in Milan as well as the Asian Championships hosted in Zhuhai, China. Though he missed the gold each time, consistent performances rocketed Vijender to the top of the world middleweight rankings in 2009. In recognition of his achievements, the same year, he was also honoured with the Rajiv Gandhi Khel Ratna.

In 2010, Vijender won the bronze medal before a cheering home crowd at the New Delhi Commonwealth Games but just a month later, went on to seize the gold medal at the Guangzhou Asian Games.

Over the next few years, Vijender got married and also toyed with the idea of making a Bollywood film. However, he soon brought back his focus on boxing and went on to win the silver medal at the 2014 Glasgow Commonwealth Games. The same year he made his Bollywood debut with the release of a film titled *Fugly*, which, however, delivered only an average performance at the box office.

Though giving up the amateur status ruled him out of the 2016 Olympic Games, with his speedy hooks and powerful uppercuts, Vijender has since had a 100 per cent win rate in professional boxing.

- In June 2015, Vijender Singh became the first Indian boxer to turn professional.
- He had initially toyed with the idea of pursuing gymnastics before he decided to go for boxing.
- Vijender has been nicknamed by the foreign press as the Indian David Beckham.

VIV RICHARDS

Famous as one of the greatest batsmen in the history of cricket, Sir Viv Richards was a dominant force in the heydays of the West Indian team. Antiguan by birth, he led the West Indian cricket team to consistent victories besides racking up an enviable Test batting average of 50.23. In ODIs too, Richards has the amazing record of winning thirty-one 'Man of the Match' awards in just one hundred and eighty seven games, which is one award every six games. Born as Isaac Vivian Alexander Richards on 7 March 1952, in St. John's in the Caribbean island of Antigua, the future batting legend grew up in a family of cricketers. His father, Malcolm Richards, was the most successful fast bowler in Antigua while his two older brothers also played for the island's cricket team. Thus, young Viv grew up playing cricket for various Antiguan clubs.

In 1973, Richards's batting genius caught the attention of the vice chairman of Somerset County Cricket Club, Len Creed, who persuaded the young Antiguan cricketer to move to England and train for the Club's team. By next year, however, Richards was sufficiently confident to make his international debut and he left with the West Indian team for Bangalore to play against India.

Very soon, Richards proved to be invaluable to the team. In 1975, Richards's consistent batting and active fielding enabled the West Indies to win the inaugural Cricket World Cup. However, it was 1976 that turned out to be Richards's finest year as he piled up a staggering total of 1,710 runs that included seven centuries in eleven Tests. His batting average that year was an unbelievable 90.00.

In 1979, again West Indies won the World Cup, primarily led by Richards's century in the finals at Lord's. Not surprisingly, Richards was selected as the captain of the team in 1984—a position that he retained till 1991. In the seven years of his captaincy, he led his team in twenty-seven victories in fifty Test matches and lost only in eight.

For many years, Richards also played for the Somerset County Cricket Club in the English County Championships. Apart from being a superlative batsman, he was also an effective fielder and off-spin bowler who compiled 32 Test wickets. However, it is primarily at the batting crease that Richards found his glory. Nicknamed the 'Master Blaster', he wowed cricket audiences across the world with his flamboyant and aggressive batting style. In 1999, he was knighted by the Antiguan government and the next year, Richards was selected as one of the five 'Wisden Cricketers of the Century'.

- In an age when fast bowlers ruled the pitch, Richards famously refused to wear a batting helmet throughout his career.

- Richards, till date, is the only captain in West Indies cricket history to have never lost a Test series.

- Indian fashion designer Masaba Gupta is Richards's daughter by Indian actress, Neena Gupta.

WANG NAN

Chinese table tennis champion Wang Nan is among the most famous female players of the sport. She is the winner of four Olympic gold medals besides winning the World Cup five times and the World Championships, a stupendous fifteen times.

Nan was born on 23 October in 1978 at Fushun in the northeastern Chinese province of Liaoning. Her first international table tennis victory came in 1994 when she won the Swedish Open. Then she went on to lift the Women's World Table Tennis Cup twice in a row—in 1997 and 1998. The next year Nan raced to the top of the ITTF rankings after having bagged the gold medal at the 1999 World Table Tennis Championships as well as the ITTF tour—in both the singles and doubles events.

However, 2000 proved to be even more successful for Nan as she swept both the women's singles and doubles categories at the Sydney Olympic Games. With these two gold medals, Nan achieved the Grand Slam of the table tennis world.

Despite a lukewarm performance in Busan where she could manage only a silver medal at the 2002 Asian Games, Nan posted a remarkable comeback the very next year. In Paris for the 2003 World Table Tennis Championships, she won gold medals in the singles, doubles and mixed doubles categories—an achievement all the more significant as it marked her third straight singles and double championships.

Not surprisingly, the next year, table tennis fans across the world had high expectations from Nan as she arrived in Athens for the 2004 Olympic Games. However, she could not defend her singles gold medal, though she won the doubles event, bagging her third Olympic gold medal. Nan's fourth and last Olympic gold medal would come in 2008 as part of the Chinese women's team's victory.

In the wake of her disappointing individual performance at the Beijing Olympic Games, Wang Nan announced her retirement from the sport. However, by that time she had already made a place for herself in the history of the sport by being inducted into the International Table Tennis Hall of Fame in 2003.

- A left-handed player, Nan is still revered for her incredible speed, loop drive and devastating topspin.
- Table tennis was made the national sport of China in the 1950s.

WAYNE GRETZKY

Canadian ice hockey player Wayne Gretzky is widely considered to be the most successful player of the sport. In a National Hockey League (NHL) career spanning twenty seasons, he has been honoured as the league's 'Most Valuable Player' an incredible nine times. And even after nearly eighteen years after his retirement, Gretzky still holds the record as the highest goal scorer in the history of NHL.

Born on 26 January 1961, in the Canadian city of Bratford, young Gretzky grew up in a family of ice hockey enthusiasts. Such was his talent for the sport that by the age of fourteen, he was already playing for the Toronto Young Nationals team after which he moved to the Sault Sainte Marie Greyhounds. In 1977, the Ontario Hockey Association voted him as the best 'Rookie of the Year' and two years later, Gretzky made his debut in the National Hockey League with the Edmonton Oilers. Largely driven by Gretzky's brilliance, the team would go on to lift the Stanley Cup again in 1984, 1985, 1987 and 1988—a feat which earned him the playoffs' 'Most Valuable Player' titles in 1985 as well as in 1988. Along with professional success, Gretzky was also popular for his clean and humane personality which led the NHL Players Association to honour him with the 'Lester B. Pearson Award' as player of the year from 1981 to 1985 and again in 1987.

In 1989, Gretzky moved to the United States and joined the Los Angeles Kings. His presence generated a lot of interest in the sport that was not traditionally popular in this west coast state. Personally too, Gretzky attained great heights and on 15 October 1989, crossed Gordie Howe's all-time points-record of 1,850. Gretzky continued with this incredible performance in the early 1990s too, receiving his tenth Art Ross Trophy as the league's leading scorer in 1994.

Gretzky played for St. Louis Blues for one season and for the New York Rangers another three seasons before retiring in 1999. In the course of a two-decade-plus career, he racked up a staggering 2,857 points besides being a top-scorer in every NHL season from 1981 through 1987, and then again between 1990 and 1994. Later Gretzky coached the Canadian national team even guiding them to a gold medal in the 2002 Winter Olympics at Salt Lake City.

- Gretzky's signature 99 jersey has an interesting anecdote behind it. Initially, he had his heart set on the number 9 jersey that used to be worn by his hero, the famous Detroit Red Wings champion Gordie Howe. However, since that was already taken, his coach suggested wearing two of the nines, and this is how Gretzky came to wear the number 99.

- In his sports career, Gretzky has captained four different teams.

WILLIE MAYS

Willie Mays was an American professional baseball player who is still considered by many experts as the best all-rounder in the history of the sport. Over the course of a twenty-two-year-long career in major league baseball, he was twice named the 'Most Valuable Player' and was inducted into the Hall of Fame in 1979.

Willie Mays was born on 6 May 1931, in Westfield, Alabama, to parents who were both into athletics. However, they separated when Willie was a child, after which he was brought up by his aunts. While studying at Fairfield Industrial High School, Willie emerged as a budding sportsman and when he was just sixteen, got selected by the Birmingham Black Barons to play on the professional Negro Leagues, though only on weekends, as he was still studying.

After graduating from high school, Mays's potential was recognized by none other than New York Giants who signed him for the minor league. These were difficult times for players of African origin as they had to face racial segregation, which meant that African American people were treated as second-class citizens (they could not drink water from the same fountain as white people or take a seat in the white area, to name a few instances). Black athletes at the time were even the target of racial taunts from the crowds. Mays however proved his mettle on the field over two seasons and his score of .477 through thirty-five games with the Minneapolis Millers, earned him a spot in the major league with the New York Giants in 1951. Mays did not disappoint and he ended the historic 1951 season—when New York Giants beat the Brooklyn Dodgers with Bobby Thomson's now-famous 'shot heard round the world' to win the National League pennant—befittingly, as the National League 'Rookie of the Year'.

After mandatory military duty, Mays returned to professional baseball in the 1954 season. He was soon leading the league in hitting with a score of .345 and a total of 41 home runs—all of which went a long way in helping the New York Giants to win the National League Championships as well as the World Series. The very next year, he smashed an incredible 51 home runs, once again leading the league.

In 1957, May moved along with the Giants to San Francisco where he wowed crowds with his hitting skills. The year 1961 saw him hitting 4 home runs in a single match while the next year, his batting powered the Giants to the World Series finals before they lost to the New York Yankees in a close finish. In 1965, Mays underlined his superstar status in baseball by racking up a total of 52 home runs that season—this would not only turn out to be his career-best but also earn him his second 'Most Valuable Player of the Year'.

After helping the Giants reach the 1973 World Cup series, May announced that he would be hanging up his baseball gloves. He retired with an enviable record of 660 career home runs, 3,283 hits and a whopping score of 2,062 runs in the course of a twenty-two-year major league career. Apart from being an excellent hitter, Mays was a highly skilled defender too, and won twelve Golden Gloves for fielding. His leaps and dives on the field to get catches, were hugely popular with the crowds and won many a match for his team. Mays's all-round skills were consistently recognized as he made it to the All-Star team twenty times in his twenty-two-season career.

Mays won hearts not only with his baseball skills but also with his humane approach. In 1979, Mays was inducted into the Baseball Hall of Fame and in 2015, he was awarded the Presidential Medal of Freedom by Barack Obama.

- Despite being a baseball star, Mays remained friendly and involved in the community–even playing stickball with kids in Harlem, which earned him the moniker, 'Say Hey Kid'.

- A part of the above phrase was eventually chosen as the title of his autobiography, *Say Hey*, which was published in 1988.

WILLIE SHOEMAKER

Willie Shoemaker is a former American professional jockey who dominated the sport of horse racing for almost three decades. For ten years in a row, his purse money totaled more than that of any other jockey in a single year and for twenty-nine years, he garnered more annual wins than any other jockey in the world. At the end of an epic forty-one-year career, Shoemaker had ridden more than 8,800 horses to victory.

Born on 19 August 1931, near Fabens, Texas, Shoemaker made a habit of overcoming hurdles right from his birth.

A hardship came Shoemaker's way when he was barely four—his parents divorced and his mother took him to live with her parents at a Texas ranch. However, it was here that the child was introduced to his destiny as he became familiar with horses and once even rode a pony unsupervised, without the help of reins or saddle.

When Shoemaker was ten, he moved to California to be with his father. Though interested in sports such as boxing and wrestling, his diminutive size would prove a hindrance to success. Frustrated, Shoemaker quit school and began looking for work in stables.

But it was only a matter of time before his real talent came to the fore. On 20 April 1949, Shoemaker won his first race on Shafter V at Golden Gate Fields and within just a year, he racked up a total of two hundred and nineteen wins.

This was just the beginning of a four-decade-plus stellar career during the course of which he dominated the Triple Crown of American horse racing which include the Kentucky Derby, the Belmont Stakes and the Preakness Stakes. Shoemaker won the Kentucky Derby in 1955, 1959, 1965 and 1986. The last victory, in fact, came when he was already fifty-four years old and with which he set the record for being the oldest winner of the event. Shoemaker went on to win the Belmont Stakes five times in his career—in 1957, 1959, 1962, 1967 and 1975. Both in 1963 and 1967, he won the Preakness Stakes as well. His victories made Shoemaker one of the highest earning jockeys and right from 1957—when he was only in his mid-twenties—he was making more than $2 million annually.

Standing at just four-feet and eleven-and-a-half-inches and weighing only 44.5 kg, Shoemaker turned his diminutive size into his jockeying strengths. His gentle hold of the horses, his tendency to ride lightly and a superb sense of pace contributed to his legendary wins. His unassuming stance on the track was accompanied by a quiet and modest personality off it.

After retiring from riding, Shoemaker got busy training racehorses. However in 1991, he suffered a motorcar accident which left him paralyzed, neck down. Even then Shoemaker did not lose purpose in life and went on to author a series of mystery novels, set in the horseracing world. He died on 12 October 2003.

- Shoemaker was a premature baby and weighed a mere 800 grams at the time of his birth—in fact he was not even expected to survive the first night of his life but his innate tenacity pulled him through.

- He was married and divorced three times.

WU MINXIA

Chinese diver Wu Minxia is the winner of seven Olympic medals—the most that anyone has ever won in the history of the Olympics. With her fifth gold and overall seventh medal in the 2016 Olympic Games, Minxia also became the winner of most individual Olympic medals in China.

Born on 10 November 1985, in the Chinese commercial hub of Shanghai, Wu Minxia took to water after watching the telecast of Chinese divers winning laurels in the Olympic Games. Young Minxia decided that this was what she wanted to do in life and started training when she was only six. By the time she was eleven, her national diving career had taken off.

Minxia's first Olympic appearance came about in 2004 at Athens. Though she won a silver medal in the 3 metre springboard category, she bagged the gold in the synchronized counterpart with Guo Jingjing as her partner. Four years later, the pair defended their gold medal before an adoring home crowd in the Beijing Olympics, though Minxia had to be satisfied with a bronze medal in the individual capacity.

Finally in the 2012 Olympic Games, Minxia defeated all competition to win her first individual Olympic gold medal in the 3 metre springboard diving event. In the same event, she again won the gold in the synchronized category, though with a new partner, He Zi.

In Rio for the 2016 Olympic Games, Minxia continued to

defend her synchronized 3 metre springboard gold medal, this time partnering with Shi Tingmao. Incredibly though, Minxia competed in only one event at Rio, she ended up breaking five world records, including winning the maximum number of medals in a single diving event as well as being the oldest female diver to win a medal in the Olympic Games.

Minxia has set multiple records in the World Aquatic Championships as well. Starting from 2001, she has won the gold medal in the synchronized 3 metre springboard event seven times besides the individual gold in 2011. The achievement makes her among the most successful divers in the history of the sport.

However, the dominance has not come easily. Minxia has had to undergo rigorous training, often going up to ten hours in a day. Also, after the 2012 Olympic Games, her father revealed that the family had withheld news of her grandmother's death and her mother's struggle with cancer so as to keep Minxia focused on her training.

Being the champion she is, Minxia has encountered all challenges with persistence and courage, rising to dominate the sport and being named the FINA 'Best Female Diver of the Year', twice in a row, in 2011 and 2012.

- Minxia has suffered numerous injuries because of which at one time, she was even nicknamed, 'Glass Beauty'.
- Before her grandmother's death, Minxia apparently made a call to her parents to ask about her health, possibly having a premonition.

YELENA ISINBAYEVA

Yelena Isinbayeva is widely regarded as the most successful female pole vaulter in the history of the sport. She is a winner of two Olympic gold medals and has won the World Championships three times. Apart from medals, Isinbayeva has several world records to her name, such as being the first woman in the history of pole vault to clear the 5 metre mark besides currently holding the world record in outdoors with a height of 5.06 metres.

Isinbayeva was born on 3 June 1982, in the Russian city of Volgograd. In 1996, young Isinbayeva caught the attention of Yevgeny Trofimov, a well-known pole vault coach in Russia, who persuaded her to give the sport a chance. So well-suited was Isinbayeva to pole vault that the very next year, she vaulted an impressive 4 metre mark.

Isinbayeva went on to win the event in the World Youth Championships for two straight years—in 1999 and 2000—and in 2001, she set new junior world records in both the indoor and outdoor events.

By the time the 2004 Olympic Games came around, Isinbayeva was already regarded as the newest phenomenon in women's pole vault. Even before arriving in Athens, she had won the 2004 World Indoor Championships. Thus, at the Olympic Games, she easily vanquished all competition with a gold-medal-winning 4.91 metres, thereby setting a new world record as well.

Next year, Isinbayeva became the first woman in the history

of pole vault to clear the 5 metre mark and also won the World Outdoor Championship. In 2006, she swept away the gold medals at the World Indoor championships, IAAF World Athletics Final as well as the World Cup.

In 2008, Isinbayeva won her second Olympic gold medal by clearing a bar set at 5.05 metres. In the outdoors category, she set a world record in 2012 by clearing 5.01 metres. However, at the London Olympics, she could win only a bronze medal. A worse fate awaited her at the Rio Olympics when allegations of the widespread state-sponsored doping programme in the Russian Federation banned all athletes from the country; Isinbayeva, who had never failed a drug test in her life, now found her 2016 Olympic medal hopes dashed and decided to retire.

However, others did not fail to recognize Isinbayeva's contribution to world athletics and in 2016, she was invited to be a part of the IOC's Athletes' Commission for an eight-year term. With as many as twenty-eight world records to her name, she has won the Olympic gold medal twice, the World Championship three times, the World Cup once, the World Indoor Championships four times, the World Athletics Final five times as well as one gold medal each at the European Championships and the European Indoor Championships. In recognition of all her achievements, she was chosen as the 'Female Athlete of the Year' by the IAAF in 2004, 2005 and 2008. In 2007 and 2009, she was also named as 'World Sportswoman of the Year' by The Laureus World Sports Awards.

- Young Yelena, like hundreds of girls from her country, initially trained to be a gymnast. However, at the age of fifteen, she shot up to a height of five-feet eight-inches, which was considered too tall in competitive gymnastics.

- In 2015, Isinbayeva signed a five-year contract with the Russian army for the post of its track and field inspector.

ZINEDINE ZIDANE

Zinedine Zidane is a former French football player who led his country to its sole FIFA World Cup championship in 1998 and European Championships in 2000. Apart from international tournaments, Zidane also had a very successful tenure with various high-profile clubs, such as Juventus FC and Real Madrid.

Born as Zinedine Yazid Zidane on 23 June 1972, into an immigrant family of Algerian origin, the future football star grew up in an under-developed neighbourhood of Marseille, known as La Castellane. Though the place was ridden with unemployment, suicide and crime, this was where he picked up the intricacies of football. When fourteen, he attended a French Football Federation training camp where his potential was recognized by Association Sportive de Cannes Football (a French association football club based in Cannes) recruiter Jean Varraud who soon inducted young Zidane into the Cannes' youth division.

After playing for Cannes and then Bordeaux, Zinedine joined the premier Italian club, Juventus FC, in 1997. This move brought him both professional and financial success. With Zidane on the team, Juventus went on to win the Italian Super Cup, a Union of European Football Associations (UEFA) Super Cup, an Intercontinental Cup, besides two more Series A titles in 1997 and 1998.

However, a far greater glory awaited Zidane in 1998. That year, France hosted the FIFA World Cup for the first time. Despite a two-match suspension awarded to him in the tournament for stepping on an opponent, he steered the home team to glory in the finals, on the wings of two fantastic goals which helped France defeat world favourites Brazil with an unambiguous 3–0.

In 2000, Zidane once again propelled France to a 2–1 against Italy to lift the European Championships Cup and was also named the 'Player of the Tournament'. The next year, Zidane moved to yet another premier European club, Real Madrid, with a reported transfer fee of $66 million plus—an unprecedented amount at the time. The French footballer promptly rewarded his new club by helping it win the UEFA Champions League title in 2002, as well as European Super Cup in the next season.

The world stage was, however, another story and France was unable to impress at the 2002 World Cup. Four years later, expectations were again high, both from the French team and its captain, Zidane. They even managed to reach the finals where Zidane scored the sole goal against Italy. However, a momentary outburst led him to headbutt an Italian footballer and consequently, he was shown the red card. Diminished in strength and morale, the French team lost in a penalty shootout to Italy. Despite the unceremonious exit, Zidane was still judged the tournament's best player and awarded the Golden Ball.

Zidane sent football fans reeling in awe with his powerful upper body moves and superb ball control which sometimes contrasted with flashes of temper. Among the most successful footballers at the turn of the century, Zidane has been thrice honoured with the FIFA 'World Player of the Year'—in 1998, 2000 and 2003. After retirement from active football, Zidane took over administrative responsibilities at Real Madrid and is currently the manager of the high profile club.

- Zidane was nicknamed, 'Zizou'.
- For scoring a goal in his debut league match in 1991, Zidane was gifted a car by his club chairman, Alain Pedretti.

ZHANG NING

Zhang Ning of China is one of the best known names in women's badminton. She is the winner of two Olympic gold medals and, more importantly, the only woman to have done so over two straight Olympic Games. Apart from her skill, Ning's experience is also what gives her an edge over newer competitors as she is among the oldest of the current female badminton champions.

Zhang Ning was born on 19 May 1975, at Jinzhou in the Chinese province of Liaoning. Her first victory at a major international competition was the 2003 World Championship where she defeated fellow Chinese Gong Ruina in straight sets.

The very next year, Ning bagged a gold medal in women's singles badminton at the Athens Olympic Games. In the finals, she defeated Dutch player Mia Audina, who had, ten years back, bested Ning at the Uber Cup finals. Along with the 2004 Olympic singles gold, Ning also found personal happiness. The same year, she married Yu Yang, who was also associated with badminton but as a coach in China.

2007 turned out to be a year of mixed fortunes for Ning who struggled to reach even the finals of several major international badminton tournaments. In 2008, with the Summer Olympics arriving in Beijing, the pressure was mounting on Ning to prove that even at thirty-three years of age, she still had a lot of play left in her. Ning did not disappoint; after a tough tournament, she reached the finals to meet the reigning World No.1, Xie Xingfang.

At the end of three gruelling sets, she was finally able to defend her singles Olympic title and with it, also set the record as the first—and till 2017—the only woman to win a gold medal in successive Olympic singles.

After the 2008 Olympic Games, Ning announced her retirement from competitive badminton, thus putting a fourteen-year international career to a close. A right-handed player, she was famous for her consistency, physical stamina as well as the ability to turn the pressure on her opponents. Currently, she coaches budding female badminton players of the Chinese national team.

- In 2006, Ning became the subject of a documentary film titled *Olympic Journey–The Road to Beijing*. It was made by famous Dutch filmmaker Roel van Dalen. Based on the life of the badminton sensation, the film popularized Zhang Ning's efforts and success on the badminton court throughout the world.

- Ning first represented China in the Uber Cup in 1994 and last represented it in 2006, making the span of her Uber Cup service, the longest by that of any Chinese player.

CONCLUSION

The great thing about sports is that it not only teaches us to win in the game but also in life. All these sportspersons have shown how passion, perseverance and hard work can help an individual overcome all possible odds—of racial discrimination, gender inequality, economic deprivation, childhood ill health, abusive upbringing and so on. Sports not only give us the mental and physical stamina to face life's challenges but even show us how to be better human beings. There are many sports icons who have turned philanthropists and are intent on giving back to the community, whether it is in the field of sports, education, health or the empowerment of disadvantaged groups—thus making the world a better place to live in, in so many ways.

ACKNOWLEDGEMENTS

I would like to thank my parents, who never stopped believing in me.

I also owe my thanks to my daughter, Kapita, who helped me make the book fun and interesting, rather than merely informative.

To my commissioning editor, Yamini, I owe my gratitude for her patience with my umpteen doubts, and also her sympathetic feedback.

And finally, to my husband, Arindam, who took care of everything else so that I could write, I want to thank you from the bottom of my heart.